The Lawyer's Guide to the Future of Practice Management

EDITED BY ALEX DAVIES

Commissioning editor
Alex Davies

Published by
Globe Law and Business Ltd
3 Mylor Close
Horsell
Woking
Surrey GU21 4DD
United Kingdom
Tel: +44 20 3745 4770
www.globelawandbusiness.com

ISBN: 978-1-78358-380-5
A catalogue record for this book is available from the British Library

Contents

Executive summary

The legal profession is changing rapidly, with increasing pressure being applied from other professional service firms, new technology making traditional services obsolete, and modern working practices changing the way in which the traditional law firm operates. Against this backdrop, it's helpful to take stock, and evaluate the way in which the future of practice management might look.

The Lawyer's Guide to the Future of Practice Management provides law firm leaders with expert opinion on the very latest guidance and market knowledge on what today's legal marketplace might look like tomorrow, organized into four crucial areas of practice management – technology, people and culture, finance and strategy – before taking a horizon-scan of the future, and what law firms need to be aware of in the coming months and years.

Kicking off the book, and the first section on technology, Simon Drane, managing director of Earlsferry Advisory, and former executive director of business development at the Law Society and LexisNexis, looks at how data will enable the shift towards the productization of legal services. The next decade will see a shift within legal service provision, where it will transition from a model that is predominantly geared around internal work processes to one geared around customer outcomes. Law firms will complete their evolution from a bill-by-the-hour service-based model to something closer to a product subscription model. This shift will deliver growth, sustainable recurring revenues at high margins, and new higher value service opportunities. At the core of this shift is the changing nature of consumption driven by consumer technology and the inexorable drive for base level information to become free. Law firms are sitting on vast quantities of data, and yet very few are currently harnessing this effectively in their offerings. The effective use of data, combined with technology, will allow innovative organizations to provide a new form of productized offering that will not only drive new recurring revenues but will also allow them to offer higher value business advisory services. Whereas effective use of data within the organization will lead to better evolutionary efficiency, quality, and risk management, the use of data in this way externally for clients will lead to more revolutionary changes. It will also blur the lines further between traditional law firms and LegalTech product businesses, in the way alternative legal service providers and the Big Four are already exploring.

Chapter two then looks at how data is transforming the relationship between lawyer and client. Jennifer Roberts, manager, strategic research at InTapp, describes how data is a great starting point and important to creating an in-depth understanding of the client – from there it's about the application of analytics, AI, and automation, along with process and people, to make the data actionable. There is plenty for legal to learn from outside the industry, taking a hard look at other professional services. However, within the industry there is progressive movement already underway, with firms hiring data scientists, adopting new technology, and transforming processes in order to better serve clients. This chapter looks at all these issues.

No book looking towards the future of practice management, in terms of technology, would be complete without some predictions around Blockchain. In chapter three, Robert Millard of Cambridge Strategy Group, looks at how Blockchain will impact law firm business models and the business of law generally. There are a number of trends (few if any involving cryptocurrencies) that intersect well with processes and systems in a "typical" law firm, and represent opportunities for improvement. This chapter goes through all these.

In part two – people and culture – Dr Bailey Bosch, director of people and culture, and Katherine Thomas, CEO at Free Range Lawyers, discuss the future of flexible working arrangements – the next stage from the "office nine-to-five". Flexible working is one way that women in particular can structure their careers to balance work and home life – but one of the biggest myths surrounding flexible work is that it only benefits the individual. If we want to see more opportunities for truly flexible working arrangements in the legal sector, the authors argue in chapter four, we need to advance the discourse around flexible work to provide a more balanced and sophisticated conversation that considers the myriad of variables that contribute to a successful "flexible working policy". Key to this is moving the discussion along from flexible working being a women's (and more specifically, a women with children's) issue and to recognize flexible work as a business tool that provides benefits at both the individual and corporate level.

Continuing with the women's theme, whilst it may have been a hundred years since the legal profession (albeit begrudgingly) welcomed women into its ranks, it often seems to have taken the best part of that century for the practice of law to find a way of accommodating them. Lawyers entering the industry today have arguably more options than ever to tread a career trajectory that doesn't end in traditional partnership, but how realistic is it that they will find, and follow, these new paths? Chapter five by Clare Harman Clark of Taylor Wessing looks at the path to partner as well as alternative trajectories such as KM and legaltech, and how there will be more opportunities than ever in the brave new world.

In chapter six, Janvi Patel, eVP, Elevate and chairwoman, Halebury, asks what good will look like in the law department of the future. Looking at five key areas – skills, creating the right culture, succession planning, the future of work, and technology – the author draws on experiences gathered from establishing Halebury, a NewLaw pioneer in the UK designed to provide genuine flexibility to corporate legal departments in meeting their legal resourcing requirements.

Chapter seven then describes how to survive and succeed leading a multi-generational practice group. Most practice group leaders would not see themselves as HR managers, but they may need to learn to think like one. Phyllis Weiss Haserot, president and founder of Practice Development Counsel, explores one of the key challenges facing legal practice leaders today – leading and motivating a multi-generational workforce to maximize productivity, engagement, and a winning client experience. She provides insight and action steps on key topics such as building multi-generational rapport and speaking with a cross-generational voice, motivating lawyers to give prompt feedback and transfer knowledge, helping young lawyers grow into leadership responsibilities, and retaining top talent.

In part three, on finance, Arthur G Greene, principal, Boyer Greene, LLC discusses how to promote firm goals through effective associate compensation approaches. Not all associates share the same career goals, and associates often serve the firm in different ways, performing different roles according to their strengths and weaknesses. In chapter eight, Arthur argues that understanding this is critical to innovating a compensation system that will maximize the contribution of associates and keep the firm financially healthy. He explains that it's not enough to simply redesign the compensation system – firms need to follow through with effective management of the compensation process afterwards, too, in order for the project to be successful.

Chapter nine offers a data scientist's perspective on law firm profitability. In the current climate, law firms are frequently encouraged to utilize innovative, technological solutions as a means of boosting profitability; in fact, factors such as the buzz at legaltech conferences mean that introducing technologies such as AI and data analytics software is now seen as critical to a firm's success. However, in a saturated tech market that exists in a state of constant flux, it is often difficult for firm management to know where and how to begin. Zev J Eigen – founder and chief science officer of Syndio Solutions – offers his expertise as a data scientist to supply two readily available forms of innovation, which embrace the possibilities technology brings and provide creative and original ways of reframing profitability.

Moving on to part four, on strategy, Christie Guimond, senior manager, legal project management, White & Case, looks at how to innovate strategically in chapter ten. Innovation is the latest trend in the legal industry and there are countless debates as to what the term means and whether there is a real imperative to innovate – the so-called "burning platform". Regardless of how you define innovation, it is clear that the industry is facing challenges related to technology disruption, changing buyer behaviors, and increasingly competitive legal markets. The degree to which these challenges are driving legal organizations to innovate varies, but many of these challenges are new for the industry, and overcoming them can require new and creative solutions. This need for creativity has caused many legal businesses to consider their approach to innovation, including who should lead it and where it should sit within the organization. Christie looks at the emerging trend in the legal industry to introduce innovation leadership models and also explores some of the potential pros and cons of each of these models. Using an example of an unsuccessful innovation leadership model from another industry, the chapter looks at how you can avoid a similar fate by using a two-part strategic planning approach for innovation that considers your current position as an organization and where you want and need to go in the future.

Chapter 11 asks "Why innovate?" Langdon Morris of InnovationLabs LLC, USA explores the link between strategy and innovation. The why of innovation is brutally simple – change is accelerating. If things didn't change, your company could keep on doing what it's always done and there would be no need for innovation. If markets were stable, if customers were predictable, if competitors didn't come up with new products and services, and if technology stayed constant, we could all just keep going as we did yesterday. But all the evidence shows that change is racing at you faster and faster, which means many new types of vulnerabilities. Technology advances relentlessly, altering the rules of business in every market it touches. Markets are not stable; customers are completely fickle; and competitors are aggressively targeting your share of the pie. So he asks: "Are we managing with the realities of change in mind? And are we handling uncertainty?" Since the alternatives are either to "make change" or to "be changed" – and making change brings considerable advantages, while being changed carries negative consequences – the choice isn't really much of a choice at all. This chapter demonstrates that you've got to pursue innovation, and you've got to do it to obtain long-lasting benefits.

Chapter 12 addresses the fundamental challenges facing any new or future leader. When starting out as a leader – especially in the legal profession, where expectations are high and hesitation or uncertainty is often construed as incompetence – it can be difficult to know how exactly to approach your management position and style. The much-discussed "imposter syndrome" is a challenge faced by many at the beginning of their management career, and a new leader may find themselves experiencing confusion and indecision when it is essential to display decisiveness and authority. Drawing from his extensive experience as an advisor and strategist, Patrick J McKenna asks the five fundamental questions confronting those entering a position of responsibility within their firm and provides guidance on the best ways to navigate them, as well as giving insight from recent research undertaken with managing partners on where new leaders spend their time – and where they *should*.

Part five looks to the future, beginning with the inevitability of multi-disciplinary practices. Michael Roster, former GC of Stanford University and formerly managing partner of Morrison & Foerster's Los Angeles office, believes that it is inevitable that lawyers and their law firms will be (in the main) replaced by highly efficient multi-disciplinary practices (MDPs) that offer bundled services and yield measurably better outcomes at a fraction of current costs. If done right, he argues in chapter 13, MDPs will be far more satisfying places to work, although lawyers may find they play significantly different roles. The question for leaders at law and accounting firms, he maintains, as well as for general counsel and other corporate executives, is whether they get ahead of the curve or find that these changes eventually are thrust upon them.

Chapter 14 takes a deep dive into the evolving role of the PSL – past, present, and future. To discern potential paths that may open up for the PSL in the future, it is critical to examine the role's past. Ailish Hogan and Lucinda Troostwyk – both experienced PSL recruiters at Taylor Root, one of the world's largest legal recruitment consultancies – explore the development of the PSL role, detailing its inception, its relationship to market conditions, and how perceptions are changing. Ailish and Lucinda proceed to then look forward, discussing the way in which career structure and progression prospects are transforming, shifting the role from a professional segue into a viable and freestanding career path of its own.

Our final chapter then looks at what the future holds for the evolving law department. Patrick J Lamb, founder of ElevateNext Law and vice president of Elevate Services proposes that legal departments should think of themselves functioning as a solar system, with the GC as the sun and the department's people and firms inhabiting an elliptical orbit dependent on which issues and tasks are prioritized. In chapter 15 he examines the practices and components that will bring a legal department closer to this innovative model and into the future, drawing from the real-world examples of Univar and Microsoft and their efforts to remain contemporary and competitive.

About the authors

Bailey Bosch is director of people and culture at Free Range Lawyers. Bailey has extensive experience in the use of psychological assessment in both organizational and clinical settings. In addition to her client work, Bailey has developed a parallel career in academia, working in university teaching and research positions for the last 15 years. A firm believer in an evidence-based approach, she is an avid consumer of psychological research and has contributed to several research groups during her career. Bailey holds a PhD in psychology and a Master of Counselling. She is currently completing her Master of Psychology in Organizational Psychology. She has membership with the Australian Psychological Society (APS) and the Society of Industrial and Organizational Psychology Australia (SIOPA) (Student) and her work is anchored in evidenced-based theories and techniques. Bailey runs her own consultancy for those organizations and individuals who wish to achieve work/life/family integration and is a regular media contributor.

Simon Drane founded Earlsferry Advisory to help people with their product strategies, whether they are technology businesses, professional services businesses, or investors. Simon has held numerous positions within the professional services sector over the last 25 years, at a FTSE 100 legal information solution provider, a legal technology consultancy, a law firm, an accounting firm, and a legal membership organization. Simon has board level experience of both executive and non-executive roles, and as CEO of a technology start-up. Simon led the new investments product strategy area at LexisNexis and created and launched many of the next generation content and workflow product offerings for lawyers. At the Law Society, Simon ran the commercial arm and also implemented a new commercial strategy that had a significant shift in focus to legal technology innovation, including the launch of a legal tech focused Barclays EagleLab accelerator.

Zev J Eigen is the founder and chief science officer of Syndio, and a data scientist focused on AI and machine learning applications in HR, labor and employment law, and legal services broadly. He was honored as one of the *Financial Times*' ten most innovative lawyers in 2016, as a FastCase50 Innovator of 2016, and as one of "40 Under 40 Rising Legal Stars" by the *National Law Journal*. He is frequently quoted in the media as an expert on Big Data solutions, predictive analytics, and machine learning, especially as applied to HR and legal services and products.

Arthur G Greene received an AB from Syracuse University in 1964 and an LLB from Boston University in 1967. He joined the law firm of McLane, Graf, Raulerson & Middleton in 1967 and became a partner in 1974. Arthur established a statewide trial practice, which focused on land use litigation, tax abatement appeals, environmental litigation, business disputes, and personal injury cases. The firm grew from 13 to 27 lawyers in four state-wide offices. He was involved in the management of the law firm from 1980 to 1992, serving during those years as a member of the management committee and as managing partner for a three-year term from 1985 to 1988. In 2000, he established a small law firm in which he practiced for a number of years. Arthur has lectured and conducted workshops, and written articles and books on a variety of law firm issues, including trends in the profession, responding to client demands, implementing alternative billing methods, marketing, leveraging with legal assistants, associate training and career development, creating and organizing effective practice groups, evaluating solutions to financial challenges, trends in partner compensation, affecting change in the law firm culture, succession planning, and preparing lawyers for the future. Arthur is a long-standing member of the American Bar Association and has served in many capacities in the ABA's Law Practice Management Section, including past chair of the section and present finance officer and liaison to the ABA Commission on the Billable Hour. He is also past chair of the ABA Standing Committee on Legal Assistants. He is past chair of the New Hampshire Bar Association's Law Practice Management Section and a past member of the Bar's Future of Law Practice Task Force. He has served on the advisory board of the Legal Assistant Management Association, is a past member of the Conference Committee of the Association of Legal Administrators, and is a fellow of the College of Law Practice Management.

Christie Guimond is a senior manager, legal project management at White & Case and the co-founder of She Breaks the Law – a global network for female leaders of legal innovation and disruption. She is also an advisory board member for a legal technology start-up, NEXL, and a legal design studio start-up, FoundationLab. Christie has over 12 years' experience working in innovation roles at global law firms, including Ashurst LLP, Hogan Lovells LLP, and Eversheds Sutherland LLP.

Clare Harman Clark is a senior professional support lawyer at Taylor Wessing LLP, building on a legal career that began over a decade ago at Clifford Chance. Before retraining as a lawyer, Clare worked as a journalist and within a government press office, and still regularly publishes articles in national and trade press. She has also been appointed as a guest lecturer in property law at the University of Westminster and sits on the Law Society's property section committee.

Phyllis Weiss Haserot is the foremost multigenerational workplace expert championing cross-generational conversation at work. She brings an unusual combination of marketing, conflict resolution, and organizational effectiveness expertise to help organizations solve sensitive intergenerational challenges that can hinder client attraction and retention, productivity, succession planning, and knowledge transfer. Phyllis is the president of Practice Development Counsel, a trailblazing business development and organizational effectiveness consulting firm she founded over 30 years ago focusing on the legal/professional services. Through her onsite, offsite, and conference programs, webcasts, "Cross-Generational Conversation" forums, monthly e-alerts and articles she has established a reputation as a "go-to" person on workplace intergenerational issues. A frequent speaker, facilitator, and blogger on intergenerational issues and business development for Forbes.com, Next Avenue, Legal Executive Institute, Huffington Post, IRIS.xyz, LinkedIn Pulse and others, Phyllis is the owner/manager of the Cross-Generational Conversation group on LinkedIn and the founder of Cross-Generational Conversation Day. Author of *You Can't Google It! –The Compelling Case for Cross-Generational Conversation at Work* (Morgan James Publishing), Phyllis is also the author of *The Rainmaking Machine* (Thomson Reuters, now in its 29th edition) and *The Marketer's Handbook of Tips & Checklists* as well as a contributor to three of ARK Group books.

Ailish Hogan qualified as a solicitor in 2002 and spent four years specializing in corporate finance before joining Taylor Root, a legal recruitment consultancy, in January 2007. Together with her colleague Lucinda – and their collective 20 years recruiting for private practice firms at

Taylor Root – she established a dedicated PSL team. They now focus on recruiting professional support lawyers and knowledge managers into a range of City, niche and West End law firms, and work with a wide spectrum of candidates, from those wishing to make their first move into a PSL role to experienced PSLs considering new opportunities.

Patrick J McKenna is an internationally recognized author, lecturer, strategist, and seasoned advisor to the leaders of premier professional service firms. His published articles have appeared in over 50 leading professional journals and his most notable book, First Among Equals (2002), topped bestseller lists in the US, Canada and Australia and has been translated into nine languages. He was recently voted by the readers of Legal Business World as one of only seven international Thought Leaders (2017).

Robert Millard is founder and a partner at Cambridge Strategy Group, a management consultancy based in Cambridge, UK, focused primarily on law and other professional service firms. Rob is past co-chair of the IBA's Law Firm Management Committee and served on the steering committee of the IBA's President's Task Force on the Future of Legal Services. He is currently busy with a doctoral research project through the Adam Smith Business School at the University of Glasgow, on value creation in large law firm mergers..

Since 2001, **Langdon Morris** has led the innovation consulting practice of InnovationLabs LLC, where he is a senior partner and co-founder. His work focuses on developing and applying advanced methods in innovation and strategy to solve complex problems with very high levels of creativity. He is recognized as one the world's leading thinkers and consultants on innovation and strategy, and his original and groundbreaking work has been adopted by corporations and universities on every continent to help them improve their innovation processes and the results they achieve.

Janvi Patel is VP, Elevated Lawyers at Elevate, where she leads flexible resourcing as a customer solution. Janvi is co-founder and chair of Halebury, an Elevate business, a leading provider of flexible resourcing solutions to FTSE 250 companies through strategic partnerships with customers such as BT, Sky, and Virgin Media. Janvi is a regular speaker at industry and business forums, Speakers for Schools and is an appointed board member on Thompson Reuters' in-house Consultation Board. She is also a board member for several non-profit organizations including Equality Now and Free Periods. Awarded an honorary degree from the University of Law in the UK for her contribution as a lawyer and entrepreneur, Janvi is a known advocate for women's rights.

Jennifer Roberts is responsible for the strategic research organization at Intapp, supporting innovative initiatives through analytics and research. Leveraging her skills to advocate, evangelize, and build data-fueled products and insight, she examines the legal industry to drive analytical intelligence that informs strategic decisions and solves organizational needs. Prior to joining Intapp, Jennifer was responsible for the innovation and development of the data and analytics thought leadership content at Thomson Reuters, working with law firms to develop insightful and actionable content as well as working internally to educate the field. Jennifer received her Masters degree from the Humphrey School of Public Policy, focusing on statistical methodology and performance measures within various industries.

Michael Roster was formerly managing partner of Morrison & Foerster's Los Angeles office, co-chair of the firm's Financial Services Practice Group worldwide, and a member of the firm's policy committee. In 1993, Mike was appointed general counsel of Stanford University, Stanford Medical Center, and Stanford Management Company. He was subsequently executive vice president and general counsel of Golden West Financial Corporation. Mike has also served as chair of the Association of Corporate Counsel, as outside director and vice chair of Silicon Valley Bank, chair of the Stanford Alumni Association, steering committee co-chair of ACC's Value Challenge, and chair of two start-up companies. He currently teaches Contract Drafting and Analysis at the University of Southern California Gould School of Law and is a director of MDRC in New York, a nonprofit organization that evaluates the effectiveness of government and other programs affecting lower- and moderate-income families and individuals.

John Sterling is chief marketing officer at Sterne Kessler Goldstein & Fox, a leading IP specialty firm based in Washington, DC. He is also the founding partner of Sterling Strategies, LLC. Prior to founding Sterling Strategies, John was a founding partner at Smock Sterling Strategic Management Consultants. He has over 30 years of experience in strategic management and market research. John has worked extensively with law and other professional service firms, as well as with industrial and consumer product companies and not-for-profit organizations. His work with TimeLine Theatre Company in Chicago won the Richard Goodman Strategic Planning Award for excellence in strategic planning from the Association for Strategic Planning. John is past president of the Strategic Management Association in Chicago and is a contributing editor to the business journal *Strategy & Leadership*.

Katherine Thomas helps legal service providers across the world grow, adapt and increase profitability with her company Katherine Thomas Consulting. With a reputation for strategic thinking combined with a large dose of pragmatism, she advises on strategy, sales, client development and the launch of new products and services. Now a consultant, speaker and coach, she previously established and led the well-known UK newlaw business Vario, a legal services provider with an emphasis on flexibility, for commercial law firm Pinsent Masons. As a result, she has a deep understanding of how alternative approaches to legal services delivery can increase competitiveness.

Lucinda Troostwyck read law at Birmingham University and qualified as a corporate solicitor in 2005 before joining Taylor Root, a legal recruitment consultancy, in 2006. Together with her colleague Ailish – and their collective 20 years recruiting for private practice firms at Taylor Root – she established a dedicated PSL team. They now focus on recruiting professional support lawyers and knowledge managers into a range of City, niche and West End law firms, and work with a wide spectrum of candidates, from those wishing to make their first move into a PSL role to experienced PSLs considering new opportunities.

Part one: Technology

Chapter 1: How data will enable the shift towards the productization of legal services

By Simon Drane, founder of Earlsferry Advisory, former executive director of business development at the Law Society, and LexisNexis

Summary

The next decade will see a shift within legal service provision, where it will transition from a model predominantly geared around internal work processes to one that is geared around customer outcomes. Law firms will complete their evolution from a bill by the hour service-based model to something closer to a product subscription model. This shift will deliver growth, sustainable recurring revenues at high margins, and new higher value service opportunities. At the core of this shift is the changing nature of consumption driven by consumer technology and the inexorable drive for base level information to become free. Law firms are sitting on vast quantities of data, and yet very few are currently harnessing this effectively in their offerings. The effective use of data, combined with technology, will allow innovative organizations to provide a new form of productized offering that will not only drive new recurring revenues but will allow them to offer higher value business advisory services. Whereas effective use of data within the organization will lead to better evolutionary efficiency, quality, and risk management, the use of data externally for clients will lead to more revolutionary changes. It will also blur the lines further between traditional law firms and LegalTech product businesses, in the way alternative legal service providers (ALSPs) and the Big Four are already exploring.

A business model in transition driven by data

Having spent the last 25 years in this space, working in law and accountancy firms and also within technology providers such as LexisNexis, I have seen real changes, but not at the scale or pace we are now witnessing. Although "design thinking" is in vogue, many traditional product businesses have worked on this basis for years, as everything is user-centered and outcome-based – if a customer doesn't feel they get a good outcome they cancel the service. At the heart of this is the need to really understand your customers' problems and deliver compelling products that solve a real need. In contrast, many professional services businesses are still trading on the process undertaken and the time it takes, along with their personal relationship, rather than the outcome. This will change as we see the generational changes in professional services changing attitudes to all aspects – from work/life balance and ownership structures to expectations of technology and the way they expect to work with their customers. People now expect easy-to-access productized solutions on their devices, and have shorter attention spans around complexity. This impact has yet to fully flow into professional services delivery models.

We are seeing a number of powerful forces that will drive real change. The generational shift, client or customer expectations, economic pressures, the overlap between tech and services businesses, and fundamentally the way in which technology can now be used in ways we couldn't imagine ten years ago, and can't predict in ten years' time. This technology revolution, much written about, will transform professional services firms. Areas such as AI and data analytics are much talked about in the legal space but so much is not yet that tangible. In accountancy though, there are some very tangible examples emerging, perhaps due to the fact that they have a head start with a very structured set of data. As Microsoft has pointed out, AI technology eats data, and what do accounting firms have a lot of? The law firms have this too, or rather a different set of it, but in many cases are not yet moving beyond viewing technology as a way of making a process more efficient as opposed to transforming a customer outcome.

This shift towards greater productization will deliver growth, sustainable recurring revenues at high margins, and new higher value service opportunities. However, it feels like 95 percent of what is emerging currently around LegalTech is focused on making processes more efficient rather than providing better outcomes. Only when law firms learn to effectively harness the data in client applications will this change. Achieving this transition requires firms to better understand the approaches and skills needed to meet customer needs and to appreciate the opportunities. There is certainly evidence of some firms embracing this; however, product management is not yet a clearly labelled investment area, and there are few that could articulate a clear product strategy. A minority of firms are starting to see the need for roles such as data scientists who really understand the data that is needed to solve client problems, where to source the data, and then how to maintain this data set.

Changes in consumption of data

In future, customers will expect to consume instantly via technology in self-serve cloud-based models, and to turn to their lawyers for higher level expertise in a more collaborative and ongoing manner. Anything that can be commoditized will be, and those smart enough will find ways to turn this to their advantage through subscription-based products. This has been the approach of information-based technology businesses such as LexisNexis and Thomson Reuters for years, as they can achieve high margins and provide an essential source of repeatable business – often referred to as subscription or "ARR" (annual recurring revenue).

The effective use of data in technology-driven productized solutions will blur the lines further between traditional law firms and LegalTech product businesses, in the way ALSPs and the Big Four are already exploring. The ALSPs and the Big Four will likely be successful in entering the legal space as they focus on processes well, understand the power of technology and of data, and are arguably more focused on how to run a profitable business and solve their clients' business problems in a holistic manner. This is the real challenge to the law firms – on the one hand they are competing with large dominant brands in the Big Four, with deep existing relationships, who have no threat of having to disrupt their existing business models in legal through a more tech-enabled "productized" manner, and on the other with very agile ALSPs who have placed an understanding of the power of data and technology at their very core.

Accountants are perhaps poised to drive significant transformation in the professional advisor space. They have the pressure of the commoditization of the audit, are naturally analytical, really understand their clients' businesses and have the key relationship with the CFO. Think about the links between a CFO and a GC in an organization and how you could possibly proactively reduce legal spend, which I think most CFOs would love. Accountants' deep relationships with CFOs, and their ability to work directly with them around areas like legal compliance to move it upstream from the GC, would make so much sense as an approach. They also hold valuable sets of data, and there is a logical fit with technology businesses such as Microsoft whose technology runs on it. Successful accounting businesses will likely become technology businesses and offer more productized solutions to clients. On top of this they will layer higher value services based on the unique insight they hold, helping their clients take more effective decisions. This transition will place them more centrally as overall business advisors and drive greater competition between accountants and lawyers.

If you are a large corporate legal department, why would you want to buy the tech and information in multiple places and then buy professional services in other multiple places if you could instead get it through one productized joined-up offering in what we used to call a "multi-disciplinary service"?

Data-driven customers driving changes

The majority of customers for law firms are corporations, which are under pressures driven in part by technology and effective data use. Understanding the customer has never been more important and law firms are beginning to place this more centrally with concepts like "design thinking". The combined buying power of these organizations with the types of technology that are emerging has the potential to dramatically transform legal service provision. Some of the LegalTech emerging on pricing and service analysis for in-house will perhaps in future drive a far greater economic dimension to the legal services model.

There is a form of supply chain review operating here that more effectively connects the real consumer (the person in the business) to the providers (the law firms). In order to get to the challenges for the legal in-house teams and then the knock-on challenges to law firms, you need to go to the start of the chain first. The underlying theme in each stage of the chain is the way in which data is transforming what is needed and can be achieved.

Firstly, business consumption of in-house legal services is evolving – the core challenge arguably starts here with the way core corporate business functions effectively interface into legal. There is clearly a shift towards things such as a single "front door" to the legal team, ensuring more accurate and efficient engagement; self-serve document automation of areas like NDAs; and better linkage to tools like Salesforce, combined with the use of electronic integrated signatures, resulting in more effective contracting. This feels like the most embryonic stage and also key to really unlocking customer pain points and identifying solutions. Technology has a key role to play here but so does understanding people dynamics and how to deliver change.

Secondly, the volume of work undertaken by the legal team has grown significantly, while in many cases costs have reduced. Technologies can improve the business of law (matter management, document management etc.) and the practice of law (document automation, process automation etc.). The legal operations function is growing, with increased focus on management information, analytics, and clear KPIs for the teams. Again, all based on data. Another key area of focus is contract management and the whole contracting lifecycle – there is currently a lack of consistency in what people are doing, even in being able to allocate the various vendors to the different stages of the lifecycle. Again, effective management of data is key, and it is important that the law firms are involved in shaping the solution. This feels like the most evolved stage of the supply chain but also perhaps the one with the biggest prizes yet to come around areas such as proper end-to-end contract management.

Finally, buying in and managing of external services from law firms is evolving – including panel management and a focus around what people are doing with e-billing and spend management software. The concept of a central instruction portal is emerging as a common theme. Some of the technology available from vendors has yet to be widely adopted, but real-time tracking of legal spend from law firms, for example, is not just of interest to the GC, but is arguably pretty interesting to the CFO, helping to better understand and predict costs. This creates both challenge and opportunity for law firms – challenge, in that it uses data to drive transparency and cost pressure, and opportunity if this data can be used to fix bigger client problems as part of a more holistic productized offering.

The ultimate customer of all this is mostly a business person in a corporate setting, seeking quicker, more predictable outcomes, and arguably whoever helps them will be the ultimate winner, whether this be a traditional law firm, an ALSP, the Big Four, or indeed a LegalTech business. How many law firms are engaging enough with their customers on their real needs (which are driven in turn by their business customers)? Perhaps they are, but it becomes challenging given their current partnership-structured, services-based business models. It appears their in-house customers may be moving faster to more productized, self-serve, data-driven, outcome-based models.

The other important aspect to consider is how clients' businesses are being challenged by technology and the knock-on effect this has for law firms. Banks, for example, are needing to transform into technology businesses in order to stay competitive. Law firms must rapidly increase tech abilities to serve their clients, with data at the heart of everything. The technology disruption for clients is driving law firms to innovate, but much of the innovation to date has been focused around internal processes rather than client delivery.

Productization underpinned by data

Consider a professional services world where data could seamlessly move between organizations. This is already being talked about between the Big Four in relation to audits, and there is no reason why this could not extend into law firms. They are already working on a common data model that would create a more secure marketplace, cut costs, and increase quality. Discussions are ongoing between law firms, audit firms, and regulators around the world on an open source approach.

A related area of interest that creates both threat and opportunity is blockchain. The basis of a large amount of legal work is contracting. The blockchain, a distributed ledger, is potentially very suited to the exchange of data housed in contracts. You enter into a contract to transact, so why not transact in a simpler way? Arguably, blockchain is the next logical step in the way contracting has evolved for lawyers, and at the very heart of this is data. Law firms that embrace this and productize offerings based on common standards can offer a new level of higher value services by using data in unforeseen ways. The efficiency created will also create threats for those that do not adapt their current processes in their service-based models.

Imagine a world with common data standards for exchange, and blockchain as a part of this underlying technology. If all clients were contracting on this, analysis of the resulting data could identify new client service opportunities. Effective use of AI technologies and data analytics on top of this could identify patterns that a human simply would not see. AI alone is not enough, but AI sitting on top of standardized data layers, with data analytics technology running on this, may allow for some breakthrough opportunities. Productizing some existing bespoke legal services with these technologies could lead to a wealth of data with which to drive higher value service offerings.

It feels like there are few examples of client data being used effectively. In the accounting space some firms are starting to shift in the way technology and data usage can transform accounting services. They are using mixed teams of accountants and data scientists to deliver higher value service offerings. They are applying statistical analysis approaches around spending data to help clients reduce costs but retain the same level of ROI. They are achieving this by combining accountancy skills, data science, and clever use of software. Bringing the rich financial data held by accountants to life in this way through effective graphical interfaces for clients in a more productized approach is allowing them to offer higher value services. Being able to proactively help clients take better business decisions will place accountants right at the center of advising clients on how to more effectively run their businesses. Accountants are effectively using approaches to move upstream in the transactional relationships they often have, away from a downstream audit to an upstream decision support approach. This is important for law firms to consider as, logically, if both they and accountants are moving up the value chain, then they will clash more in the future.

Lawyers must ask themselves what the client really wants. Automation is not enough, they want transformation. How many of them want a lawyer as opposed to the outcome a lawyer can deliver for them? How many of them care about the process undertaken rather than the end result? Clients really care about who can deliver an outcome. If, for example, a law firm has created a legal dashboard for the GC that allows the business to self-serve through a common front door, the GC to allocate resources and the CFO to monitor various KPIs, then it will be able to engage in more strategic conversations with the corporation around decision-making. It will then be able to offer higher value business advice on top of this through the unique insight it holds, irrespective whether it is technically a legal matter. At the core of achieving this will be the way in which law firms productize the valuable data they hold.

Once all data has been systematized, sitting on blockchain, with AI running over the top, delivered in more productized forms, it's not hard to imagine things like self-executing contracts. So much of what lawyers do is managing risk, and if there are automated ways to do this that would seem appealing. Clients would achieve greater risk and time benefits and be able to consume this in a simpler form. Would a client care that they were paying for a productized solution rather than a lawyer billing them by the hour? Wouldn't they rather have the lawyer provide a higher-level advisory service sitting on top of a more productized offering when they need it?

You may think this shift towards productization underpinned by data sounds highly unlikely, argue that many areas cannot possibly be viewed in this light, and that there will always be a need for the trusted advisor, especially around those "bet the farm" transactions. I agree. However, these areas will logically shrink as more and more becomes productized by either the technology providers or the innovative firms that look hard at what they do and really question how much of it is genuinely unique or bespoke. Also, in this drive towards productization there will be new higher value advisory offerings that will emerge, but logically only those that have embraced productization will be able to offer these. The barriers to achieving productization of services are perhaps the partnership structure of many firms and the need for investment capital. Where this is a profitable partnership model it can be hard to persuade people to invest for the long-term.

But what about the product vendors who have long understood that the real underpinning of their models is data. The Microsofts and the Thomson Reuters, that came from a background of building strong data sets and finding profitable business models to leverage this through technology. How will these product businesses react as services firms adopt increasingly productized approaches for the same customers?

As an example, Microsoft has a compelling set of tools to help accountants in transforming their clients' businesses and are offering to act as the hub and help connect up their technology implementation partners with their accounting partners to jointly help their shared clients achieve new insights. This makes so much sense, given the key challenge to leveraging some of the transformative technology is access to quality sources of data. Who better has high quality structured data sets of business information than the accountants? Microsoft feels that the move to the cloud, through Azure, has enabled a lot of this to become a reality in a cost-effective way. It sees a shift towards more productized subscription-based services that then become a reality of what accountants will provide. In its view, AI is not a technology play but rather a transformation play and this shift in delivery model is what the transformation delivers. But what of the role for law firms in this race to effectively use data to drive higher value offerings, and who also are heavy Microsoft users? How quickly can law firms move to more structured data models and productized client offerings?

A challenge for law firms as they move towards productization is therefore how they will work with these technology providers – in partnership or in competition. Providers such as LexisNexis and Thomson Reuters have been on a long journey of commoditizing or rather productizing the law through the tools they provide lawyers. Take an area like legal analytics, that didn't even exist five years ago, and think about the data that clients can now access to aid decision-making where they may have relied on advice from the law firm in the past. How law firms determine their product strategy will be crucial.

There is also a challenge currently in the way law firms are viewing innovation within their operating structures, with the label applied to many things that are not really that innovative for the client. If they were a product business, innovation would be a value, not a team, and the team that drives a lot of the strategy would probably be the product team. In professional services currently there is not yet a consistent view of the role of the "product manager", or the need for a product strategy, but this will change. How long before law firms have chief product officers on the board? I think we are at a point for many where they are starting to see the distinction between the CIO and the CTO roles but possibly not yet what may come next in the form of the CPO role.

Conclusion

Professional services firms are undergoing a shift in moving towards a greater degree of technology-enabled productization, and need a clear data and product strategy to ensure success. At the center of this is the need to better understand client problems, and the essential role that data plays. Law firms need to develop a clear data strategy and build new skills, but also need to go beyond this and define a clear product strategy around how this data will power new productized revenue models, which lead to higher value service opportunities. They need to do this quickly as they have increasing competition on many fronts from organizations that have put an understanding of data and technology at their very core.

This chapter originally appeared in *Building the data-driven law firm*, published in June 2019.

Chapter 2:
How data is transforming the relationship between lawyer and client

By Jennifer Roberts, manager, InTapp

There has been plenty of writing on the ways in which legal must change – the increased competition from in-house and new entrants in the market, consolidation of firms, the constant threat of lateral moves from individuals to entire practices and a more sophisticated client all make for mounting pressure at firms of all sizes. These pressures aren't all that different from those that other industries have faced. Looking at the professional services industry, accounting is experiencing these pressures as well – including the fall of the Big Five, as Arthur Andersen LLP folded in the early 2000s, the commoditization of work with the advent of e-filling, and accessibility of AI-infused technology to eliminate the need for tax oversight as well as regulations increasing. The answer for large accounting firms over the last 20 years has been to transform the traditional business model to compete in new ways and even new industries. Look at the investment accounting is making in legal. PwC, Deloitte, EY, and KPMG snagged top spots on Acritas' 2018 list of global brand alternatives.[1] Outside of professional services, airlines, phone companies, and hotel chains have all transformed their business models in order to compete.

One thing that all of these transformations have in common is that, at their core, they've leveraged data and technology to win. For the Big Four it has been about new ways to deliver services and investments in things like legal technology to drive alternative services and expand their client base. For airlines, hotels, and phone companies, it has been about strategic investments to help become client-centric, implementing technology and collecting data to help deepen client relationships.

How is data being used?

But what does this mean? How is data actually being used in other industries to revolutionize the business model and change the relationship between client and business?

Client health

There has been a proliferation of data and analytics that sit on top of customer relationship management (CRM) systems to provide scores similar to credit ratings and grades to help businesses understand their relationship with their clients. Scoring offers dimensions to a relationship, which are the basis of the calculus. The score takes into account revenue, number of products owned, sentiment, interactions, number of contacts, age of client – the list goes on. These dimensions help businesses understand what it means to not just be a good client but also – equally as important – a bad one, helping businesses triage where needed. A client with a strong health score is less likely to attrite and has an increased propensity to continue to purchase, equating to higher revenue from happy clients. In cases of the opposite, it becomes actionable as a business can look at what levers to pull to improve the relationship and decrease the chances of attrition, perhaps even expanding the client's footprint once remedied.

Client experience

Client experience has taken a big step forward in most industries with the advent of a more sophisticated consumer. Understanding interactions between the organization and customer is now measurable with data. Seventy-eight percent[2] of businesses are using client experience as a market differentiator to compete and win as client experience has been shown to decrease operating costs and increase revenue through reduced attrition, building strong client relationships, and winning new business.[3] Metrics include the number of touchpoints along the customer journey to net promoter score, customer satisfaction, and customer effort and response time. All of these data attributes are collectable through automation and triggered workflows to kick-off an email once the consumer has made a purchase or the work is done to ask if they would recommend the business to a friend (NPS) or even short sentiment surveys at different points in the lifecycle. Positive customer experience means more sales as well as positive word of mouth, aka references. When it comes to overall financial performance, the Temkin Group's 2017 State of CX Management report[4] showed that 73 percent of companies with above average customer experience have better financial performance than their counterparts with less mature customer experience programs (only 44 percent saw strong financial performance).

Upsells and cross-sells

Leveraging data to segment audiences, predictive models, and machine learning can gain insight into where to cross- and up-sell. Advanced analytics can recommend products and services to similar clients based on buying bundles. Influencing sales with data and AI provides a more personalized shopping experience for customers and helps to improve the customer experience. Predicting an opportunity can help to anticipate the needs of clients, transforming the process from reactive to proactive.

Sales process

Client data, in combination with AI, is transforming the relationship between client and sales professional, allowing sales to move beyond intuition and leverage data to bolster decision-making. According to McKinsey Global Institute,[5] 45 percent of activity can be automated allowing for professionals to uplift their time and bring additional value to more strategic and proactive activities to nurture the relationship. Not only that, professionals can now pursue the right leads with confidence through predicting opportunities as mentioned above. This is based on rich client profiles from data around the business. It is no longer about guessing if the client is a good match for the product, rather about intelligently predicting. This all lends a hand in smoothing the sales process through an effort of collaboration between data, AI, and the professional.

Data at the firm-level

The correlation between data-driven client relationships and revenue cannot be ignored. The analyses above are just a few examples of how other industries are realizing their potential through data-driven client relationships. According to Forrester Research,[6] hotel chains have reaped the biggest benefit to data-driven relationship building (through customer experience), gaining $1.364 billion of revenue, a majority of which ($825 billion) can be attributed to retaining business that could have been lost to competitors. Additionally, hotels with above average client experience have the potential to earn a cumulative $495 million in revenue from additional purchases.

Realizing these concepts are ahead of legal, the data train is moving. Understanding the concepts and basic principles around the type of data to capture, and how to leverage it, can offer a foundation so that legal does not need to start from scratch. There are plenty of signs to where the bets are being placed in legal. Anecdotally, data and AI is touted at conferences in the many ways it is transforming the business model.

The legal technology industry is booming, with start-ups focusing on data-centric applications. In 2018 alone they raised more than $1 billion in funding, with more than a third of that amount focused on artificial intelligence applications and the use of data.[7]

In a recent survey in collaboration between Intapp and Law Vision titled "The rise of the legal data scientist",[8] more than 80 percent of survey respondents indicated that they felt the data analytics function was useful and 70 percent found it to be extremely or very valuable (see Figure 1). However, only 53 percent of responding firms incorporate data and analytics into their overall strategies. A clear misalignment exists between perceived usefulness and value for the 27 percent of firms that find data analytics useful but don't incorporate it into strategy. However, some firms are reaping results by having alignment, making the investment in data and data experts, and are implementing a strong data story across the firm. Specifically, more than 50 percent of the firms in the survey with positive revenue growth in 2018 employed a data scientist or plan to do so within the next 12 months, suggesting a data culture and analytics posture beyond the basics. Additionally, firms with revenue growth identify the value of analytics to be extremely valuable for 52 percent, as compared to only 16 percent of firms with neutral or negative revenue growth. While correlation isn't causation, there is certainly a case to be made for those innovating with data.

Aside from aligning value, usefulness, and strategy, what are law firms doing?

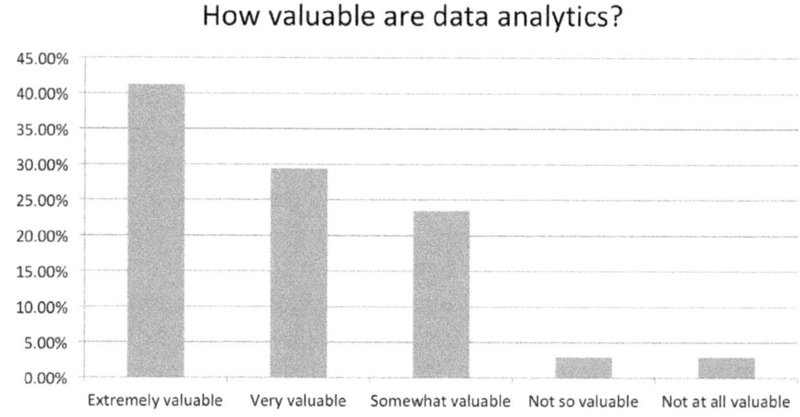

Figure 1: How valuable are data analytics? Source: Intapp and Law Vision: "The rise of the legal data scientist".

Figure 2: Are data analytics part of your firm's strategy? Source: Intapp and Law Vision: "The rise of the legal data scientist".

Five years ago, firm rosters rarely included titles like data scientist or chief analytics officer. Now these roles, at all levels, are proliferating within firms. According to ILTA's 2018 Technology Survey, the analyst role has grown rapidly, in some instances even surpassing headcount for security staffing. There are many new titles within firms from analyst to data scientist.

Data scientists – defined as data wranglers who consume mass amounts of messy data, be it structured or unstructured, and apply skills in math, statistics, and programming to clean, manage and organize data into insights, feedback systems, and automation – are a newer breed within firms. Over 20 percent of respondents to the "Rise of the legal data scientist' survey had a data scientist on staff, with another 12 percent planning to hire in the next 12 months. A majority of these data scientists entered the law firm within the last year or two. Related to the data scientist is the analyst, arguably individuals who have paved the way for their data science counterparts. Analysts are defined as individuals that provide answers to business problems through data, primarily focusing on what happened and why it happened. They define, analyze and document insight in order to develop solutions. This group spans business development, KM/research, business intelligence, operations, and finance. While the analyst primarily reports into the chief financial officer (CFO), the data scientist is embedded in different areas across the firm (see Figure 3), primarily dependent on the initiatives in which the data scientist is supporting.

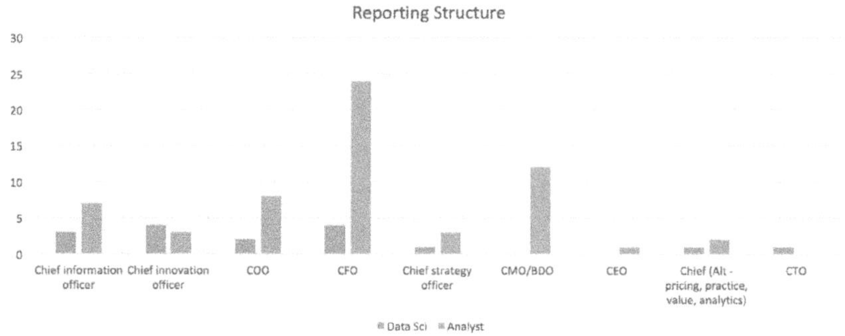

Figure 3: Reporting structure. Source: Intapp and Law Vision: "The rise of the legal data scientist".

Investing in resources is just the beginning in terms of leveraging data to drive client relationships. With the people in place, questions remain around data and process.

Data, data, data

There is certainly no shortage of data within law firms. In the 2018 Growth Enablement Survey, undertaken in collaboration between Intapp and Calibrate Legal, participants were asked what internal data elements they commonly use in business development activities. The usual suspects make the list – as shown in Figure 4. The top five data points – practice, service types, lawyer data, matter description, and industry codes – help to understand the client's needs and how the firm is delivering value. But there is so much more potential. Attributes such as client longevity and time spent by relevant teams with the client are easily captured data elements that can lend a strong hand into understanding the client, yet they aren't used with frequency. Client longevity can be as simple as when the first engagement began, pulled from time and billing systems. Relevant teams – again pulled from time and billing systems – provides an understanding of all those who have "touched" the client per matter. These elements are just a few examples of data already available to help paint a more holistic picture of the client.

Some data isn't as straightforward to capture but is vital to helping a firm measure the relationship between client and firm. Things like satisfaction are important data elements, as evidenced in other industries, but are not always easy for firms to capture. The relationship partner might not want to collect this information, and it can also be tricky to get clients to respond. However, data that is already collected at the firm can step in as a proxy variable. Proxy variables are used in the practice

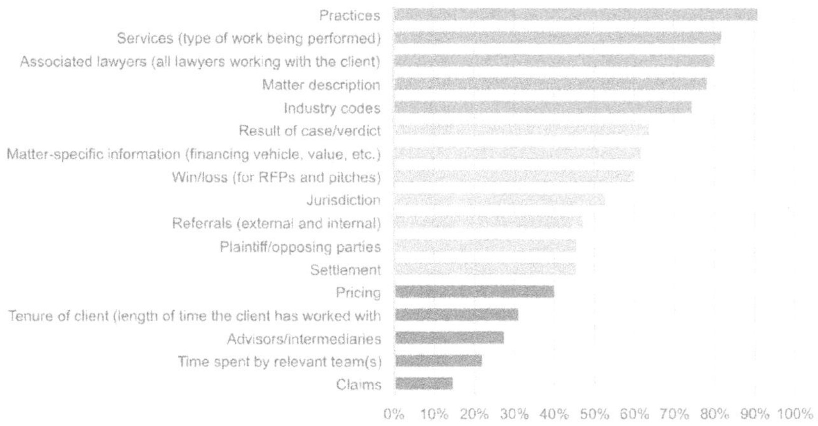

Figure 4: Internal data elements commonly used in business development activities. Source: 2018 Growth Enablement Survey, Intapp and Calibrate Legal.

of data science to capture indirect measures of a desired outcome. It is common practice when direct measures cannot be obtained or they are unobservable. In the case of client sentiment, a combination of variables can be used to define the client's attitude towards the firm, including:

- Client longevity (the longer a client has been with a firm actively engaging in matters suggests loyalty);
- Number of relationships at the firm (the more relationships a client has at the firm beyond just the relationship lawyer suggests a connection with the firm – something that is ideal in the age of lateral movement);
- Number of practices engaged (when three or more practices are engaged, a client has a higher propensity to purchase additional services, a suggestive variable regarding the state of the relationship with the client as an unhappy client would not continue to engage work); and
- Realization (realization is linked to value. Value can be allusive and is defined differently by all but a client who sees the value in the work being done will have stronger realization as they are willing to pay).

All of these attributes brought together into a composite health score provide a picture of client sentiment.

Deriving variables is yet another methodology used frequently in data science. This is the creation of new variables to measure things that aren't currently being measured (rather than things that are difficult to measure, which is where proxy variables shine). One example of a derived matter is the duration of a matter defined as how long a matter lasts. Trending duration across clients can help understand how the firm may better serve similar clients and help find efficiencies. Another example is effort, as in the rhythm of a matter. This gets at what roles are taking part at what point. Are associates doing the upfront work and partners on the backend? Or is it reversed? Is it mixed? Effort can help the firm understand the types of matters and how best to serve and staff clients based on the matter and type of client.

While there is plenty of internal data available at the firm to leverage at face value and even develop new metrics, there is an ample supply of external data to secure a robust data set on the client. When asked what external data sources are currently being used at the firm for client endeavors, market benchmarking data such as Peer Monitor and ALM were used by over 50 percent of respondents to "The rise of the legal data scientist survey". This data is helpful when it comes to competition and winning work for peers. Other external data such as Dunn and Bradstreet and consumer data offer demographics on the client such as industry, corporate trees, revenue, and number of employees. When this data is combined with the internal data already discussed, it can aid in analyses around segmenting to understanding buying patterns for similar clients. Once segmented, firms can define how to meet similar clients' needs and what makes a client sticky (aka loyal).

Leveraging data into actionable client analytics

With a strong hold on the data at the firm's disposal and expertise to help tell the story, process, including the right methodology, is necessary to analyze and operationalize. The popular types of analyses shown in Figure 5 are what analysts and data scientists at the firm are currently spending their time on. Thinking in terms of Gartner's analytics maturity model, law firms are still very early on when it comes to the analytics being used, with 89 percent of respondents to *The rise of the legal data scientist* survey playing primarily in the descriptive and diagnostic phases, answering the questions of what happened and why did it happen? This is informative when it comes to understanding the client but it also requires a lot of human input to get to a decision and action. As you move down the maturity model these aspects lessen to make the analytics actionable faster with less human input.

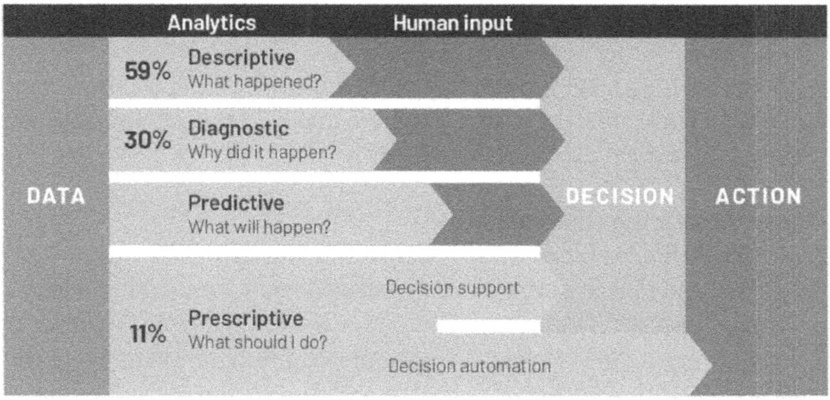

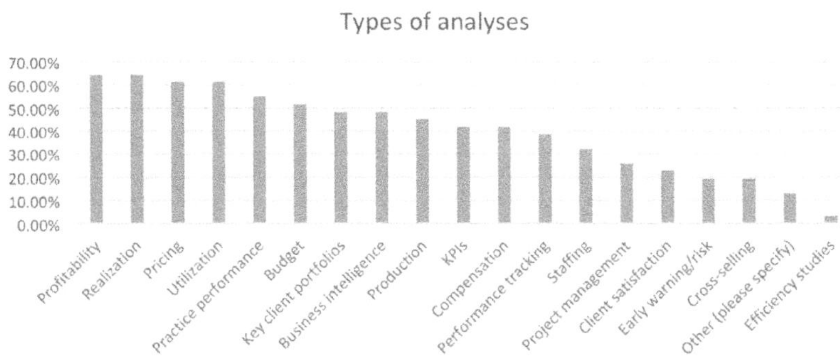

Figure 5: Popular types of analyses. Source: Intapp and Law Vision: "The rise of the legal data scientist".

Within the descriptive and diagnostic space, analyses are used principally for financial modeling to understand performance, investment, and debt. Analyses like project management, client satisfaction, early warning and cross-selling are happening but with less popularity. It is these analytics that truly help to win the work and get to the heart of the client, which render the highest ROI as evidenced in other industries. Based on "The rise of the legal data scientist" survey, this is likely due to limited resources and lack of data in pertinent areas to ensure a robust analysis.

Despite the focus, operationalizing these analyses is a hurdle. A majority of the work remains static, with over 60 percent of respondents to the data scientist survey reporting that these are run on demand. Automation in reporting is seen for less than 10 percent; moreover, only 12 percent of respondents are embedding this work into the firm's work stream, making it easily assessable. It is no wonder there is misalignment between strategy and usefulness, if the analyses aren't even being used. Yet, this is a hurdle firms must cross, along with moving down the maturity model of actionable analytics laid out by Gartner. Firms must move to actionable analytics that help to define and drive client relationships in order to realize the potential of data and the revenue opportunity evidenced in other industries.

Operationalizing innovation

There are firms overcoming the hurdles and moving into the space of predictive and prescriptive analytics that are operational and helping to drive relationships. These are the analytically postured firms, with more than 50 percent positive revenue growth, according to "The rise of the legal data scientist" survey.

What does a strong data posture at a firm look like? It comes down to people, process, and data. Firms making headway are investing in the right people (data scientists and analytically minded leaders) and working across the firm when it comes to process. Client-centric analytics projects cannot happen in a vacuum – the data is all around the firm and so is the power of making it work. Functions that touch the client such as intake, conflicts, pricing, and finance, in conjunction with business development and marketing, have the power to join forces and impact the way the firm interacts with the client when bringing in new work.

A space for innovation

Frequently the act of proposals, pitches, and RFPs is done reactively and without foresight for profit or firm strategy. Chasing poor opportunities is a frequently discussed concern by business development as it requires a big effort on their part, resulting in very little reward in some cases. Understanding that not all work is about profit, and some work is brought in to grow or strengthen relationships, is a tried and true tactic but this is far more the exception than the rule. To ensure pursuance of the right work requires collaboration and re-engineering the process. The intake and conflicts team can be brought in to not just access the potential conflict of a client or matter but also assess if a client or matter is viable from a financial standpoint in terms of profit and that the client doesn't have a risk of carrying bad debt. This also provides an opportunity to ensure that the work aligns to the firm's strategy (perhaps in a practice or industry the firm wants to expand their relationship). If the work doesn't make sense for the firm, isn't profitable, or is with a client carrying debt, it doesn't make sense for the firm to pursue the work. Part of winning this work is pricing. Business development, marketing, and pricing can come together to use client analyses such as segments to guide the best way to price and position a proposal that increases the chances of winning the work and offering a competitive rate.

Once won, intake and conflicts already has an idea for the work and it has been cleared on all measures. Additionally, a price has been agreed upon, thus the value of the work is known. When the work has started, business development, marketing and pricing have an understanding of what is being delivered and can monitor it with financial data, tracking the progress and helping the lawyer and client to ensure delivery of value and satisfaction. By understanding who the client is, the agreed upon work and what successful engagements look like by similar clients (all provided through data), the firm is upping the game in how the client is being served, therefore deepening the relationship.

There is also an incredible data synergy here, as intake and conflicts are pulling external data to get at corporate trees and relationships as well as information on the client and related parties. Marketing and business development bring more to the picture with the firm's expertise, how clients have been served through leverage, longevity, and lawyer teams. Finance and pricing help fill in any gaps around structure of work, profit, revenue, and hours.

As if winning the work and delivering value was not enough, leveraging this data can help a firm become proactive in client relationships. This data all lends a hand into developing a client profile. Profiling clients lends to segmenting similar clients, understanding buying patterns and, in more sophisticated examples, predicting and forecasting white space to anticipate needs.

Conclusion

The example above is the ultimate state of a client-centric business model driven by data. During the era of big data, other industries have paved the way to provide ideas on the potential of driving relationships through data for firms to leverage. Firms are taking note and biting off small pieces to begin the journey to transform the business model that embraces data and transforms the relationship between firm and client. Signs of firms embracing data include hiring data scientists and leveraging analyses beyond the comfortable KPIs. It is the next leap that might be the hardest as it requires a cultural shift to a data posture. While data is at the bottom of all of this, people and process play a big role in making this actionable. This doesn't just require hiring data-minded experts, but also getting other professionals and lawyers to play, allowing functions to collaborate for the sake of the client. The end game is realizing a better market position to not just compete but also retain and grow clients through strong client relationships.

This chapter originally appeared in *Building the data-driven law firm*, published in June 2019.

References

1. www.acritas.com/global-alternative-legal-brand-index-2018.
2. Econsultancy. (2015, January). Quarterly Digital Intelligence Briefing: 2015 Digital Trends. Retrieved from https://econsultancy.com/reports/quarterly-digital-intelligence-briefing-2015-digital-trends/
3. Manning, H., & Bodine, K. (2012). *Outside In.*
4. https://blog.lawgeex.com/legaltech-hits-1-billion-investment-as-lawyers-embrace-automation
5. https://temkingroup.com/product/state-cx-management-2017/)
6. www.mckinsey.com/business-functions/digital-mckinsey/our-insights/four-fundamentals-of-workplace-automation."
7. Manning, H., & Bodine, K. (2012). *Outside In* (p. 30).
8. www.intapp.com/insights/the-rise-of-the-legal-data-scientist/

Chapter 3: Blockchain's likely impact on law firm business models

By Robert Millard, director, Cambridge Strategy Group

The promise of distributed ledger technology (Blockchain) is to deliver a radically different world – one without a need for intermediaries. Governments, banks, and many others whose *raison d'être* relies on an intermedial function, or on the continued global pre-eminence of fiat currencies, are right to be nervous. The vigor with which Blockchain developers and users pursue that promise in coming years will depend, in no small measure, on how such intermediaries can make their services more efficient, affordable, and user-friendly, probably by themselves using Blockchain applications and almost certainly combined with artificial intelligence (AI).

Triggered by a wave of speculation in cryptocurrencies that peaked at the end of 2017, the second half of that year saw several regulators around the world cracking down on cryptocurrencies and initial coin offerings (ICOs.) Some governments even hinted at banning them, although as Jens Weidmann (president of the Deutsche Bundesbank and chairman of the Board of the Bank for International Settlements) has noted most presciently: "Seeing as transactions of this kind are offered worldwide, there's only so much that a national or European regime can achieve".[1] In short, for cryptocurrencies to be comprehensively regulated, all countries in the world would need to agree a common set of regulations. Such consensus constitutes an unlikely scenario. Some countries, including several in the Middle East, have even openly stated intent to enhance their global competitiveness by transforming their economies to align with emerging global digital trends, including a very heavy focus on Blockchain and cryptocurrencies.

Several large retail banks have adopted measures to make it more difficult for their customers to use their services to acquire and sell cryptocurrencies. On the other hand, some central banks have intimated that they will likely start issuing cryptocurrencies themselves, in which case retail banks will need to develop products around those. We've also seen several global securities exchanges launch Blockchain-based platforms.

Cynics scoff at the supposed lack of substance behind cryptocurrencies, the vast amounts of energy that it requires to maintain them, and the risk of investments being hacked. They also point out (correctly) that many proposed Blockchain applications can be hosted just as effectively and far more efficiently on centralized databases, in the cloud or otherwise. The hype that surrounds the topics of Blockchain and cryptocurrencies at present has done little to enhance market understanding of either their potential, or the threat to the status quo. Transformational impacts will furthermore probably not result from Blockchains alone, but Blockchains acting together with other digital disruptions such as AI, the Internet of Things (IoT), big data, and advanced "5G" (and beyond) wireless networks.

Most of all, the focus on cryptocurrencies as a highly speculative asset class has drawn attention away from the Blockchain feature that offers the most radical, disruptive innovation. That is, the promise for parties to even quite complex transactions to deal directly with each other, without the need for cumbersome and frequently expensive intermediaries. This feature is not incidental. It is the central theme of the paper published by Satoshi Nakamoto (who is yet to be identified) in 2009, at the height of the global financial crisis.

What is certain is that the somewhat clunky Blockchains of today will evolve in sophistication and scope in coming years. It is always dangerous to predict the future of an emergent trend from its early manifestations. Motor vehicles in the late 19th century gave little indication that they would, within just a few decades, completely replace horse-drawn transport. Many at that time scoffed at the new automobile technology, in a similar way to how some today dismiss Blockchain. Yet some proponents of Blockchain technology portray it as representing an entirely new generation of the Internet, with a network of Blockchains poised to co-exist alongside the World Wide Web, allowing users to transact as well as store and share information and communicate as they do via websites and social media applications.

The degree to which Blockchains deliver on this promise of radical, disruptive transformation of commerce and trade depends on how quickly new versions of Blockchain technologies or applications emerge that better meet the needs of ordinary users.

Consider, for instance, a wine farmer in Argentina, who wishes to sell a container-load of wine to a merchant in Japan. Traditionally, such a transaction would involve a complex set of actions (on which the international trade practices of law firms have thrived) and transactions (which have similarly been important sources of revenue for banks.) Blockchain applications and smart contracts already exist that make it possible for the parties to transact directly with each other, without the need for credit checks or other safeguards to create inter-party trust.

That transaction would also traditionally have been denominated in one of the world's global reserve currencies – most commonly US dollars. The wine merchant would have instructed his bank to pay the funds in dollars into the bank account of the wine farmer, paying for those dollars with yen. The farmer's bank would then have converted the dollars into Argentinian pesos. Each step in such a transaction attracts bank charges and sometimes involves delays, even errors. Blockchain removes the need to use an intermediary fiat currency at all. It is easy to speculate that if such practices became widespread, they could reduce the demand for dollars and other reserve currencies, reducing the value of those currencies. Although tax authorities can monitor the flow of funds at the intersections at which fiat currencies are converted into cryptocurrencies (and vice versa) it is also easy to see how it would be possible for the parties to hide the transaction partially or wholly from the tax authorities. Such behavior would, of course, be illegal. However, there seems little doubt that the advent of Blockchain already makes tax compliance monitoring and enforcement more complex.

In early 2018, I advised a major international accounting and tax advisory firm, on a project to visualize what an international tax practice might look like in 2025. Blockchain and AI were fundamental to this discussion. It seemed an inescapable conclusion that Blockchain applications would be far more prevalent in 2025. Also, that Blockchains could and likely would be used to conduct business outside of the view of the tax authorities. In turn, those authorities would need to turn to Blockchains and AI themselves, to protect tax revenues and to monitor and enforce compliance. Legitimate and serious concerns also exist about the potential for cryptocurrencies to be used for money laundering, funding illegal activities and, where relevant, circumventing currency control regulations.

At its core though, is remains that Blockchain promises no less than a fundamental reimagination of commerce and industry – perhaps even the functioning of human society.

If that hypothesis is correct, then the impact on law firms will probably also be transformational, including in ways that we cannot begin to conceive of from today's perspective. How firms should deal with this needs to focus less on trying to forecast these impacts and more on dealing with that uncertainty itself. Very soon, we can expect mainstream discussions around Blockchain technology to expand to include the characteristics of a distributed-ledger, multi-Blockchain world. How will transactions of all kinds work, in such a world? What institutions will be required and how will they need to operate? What safeguards will be necessary and how will these be ensured? Will existing intermediary businesses be able to reinvent themselves to ensure continued relevance in that world? How will client needs be different? What law firm strategies and business models will best meet those needs and deliver high performance? It may take three, five, or more years for these questions to become mission-critical – or it might happen in the next 12 months. We don't know. We don't even have enough substantive information about how this will unfold in practical terms, to build more than the most superficial of scenarios. Under the conditions of uncertainty and hyper-competition that characterize legal services today, it is even more critical for effective strategic decision-making, to have meaningful insight not only about what is currently happening in the market, but also about what will likely come next.

In order to build a basic understanding of how Blockchains are likely to impact the business models of law firms, it is useful to consider three perspectives, namely applications that:

- Affect legal needs and so translate into new service opportunities for law firms;
- Present opportunities to enhance efficiency, performance, and security (especially cybersecurity) of business models and processes within law firms; and
- Compete with law firms by offering solutions that render services they currently provide redundant (especially services that are intermedial rather than advisory in nature).

Impact on client legal needs

Law firms are generally reactive to clients' legal needs, so it follows that practices focused on servicing client needs associated with Blockchains will develop well beyond their current nascent state. Blockchain applications are now appearing in almost every industry sector definable and while the impact on some is only marginal, on others it seems likely to be radically disruptive. Some of the most immediate developments that one might expect to see advance in 2018/19 include those listed below.

Trade finance

Financial institutions, logistics companies, and shipping fleets are all experimenting with Blockchain to create smart contracts, to reduce the administrative burden and costs involved in trading – especially but not only across international borders. Supply chain management is an obvious adjunct to this. In trade finance, Blockchain addresses the relatively high cost of transferring funds across currencies (especially low-value payments.) The transparency and immutability of the records on Blockchains remove the need for parties to trust one another.

Financial services and Fintech

While more standardized financial products like swaps and other derivatives seem ripe for conversion to Blockchain platforms, it is unlikely to stop there. Lack of uniformity across documentation will make some areas more difficult, but AI is getting better at dealing with resultant ambiguities. As these tools get better, and as the cost and time savings become apparent, so we can expect documentation used with such products to become more uniform. More and more areas of financial services will become ripe for conversion to Blockchain platforms.

Of course, companies that develop Blockchain applications frequently fall into the Fintech industry sector themselves and opportunities exist for lawyers to grow practices that focus on their unique legal needs, too.

Other business needs

By mid-2017, research by UK-based Juniper Research showed that 57 percent of large corporations polled (>20,000 employees) were either actively considering or in the process of deploying Blockchains. Two-thirds of companies surveyed said that they expected the technology to be integrated into their systems by the end of 2018. It is highly likely that some of these applications will create new, unanticipated legal needs for those corporations, and that they will not yet fully understand those needs and how to meet them. Given the transactional nature of the relationship between most law firms and their clients, it is unlikely that those law firms have any better insight into the matter. Put differently, in the absence of what in other industries would be called "research and development", most law firms have abysmally poor insight into many of the services that they will need to be selling to clients, even in the medium-term.

Opportunities to enhance efficiency and performance within law firms

Blockchain applications and tools developed specifically for law firms are so far scarce, but they are beginning to make an appearance. Workflow automation software that automates business processes and creates audit trails (e.g. ThinkSmart and BlockAudit) is starting to make an appearance, mostly in high-tech legal departments. Blockchain-based platforms are also being developed to manage version control across the multitude of documents and other records that law firms routinely produce. During the 2018 "Global Legal Hackathon", London-based Pinsent Masons fielded a team that developed a Blockchain-based application to manage the workflows around the exploration of innovative ideas that emerge in their firm and for partners to vote on which ideas should receive investment and be implemented. With most LegalTech investments still going to eDiscovery-related applications, Blockchain applications appear to be neglected for the moment. One should not underestimate the ease with which Blockchain applications developed for other industry sectors can be retooled to meet the needs of a law firm, however.

Adapting to Blockchain technologies may, in the end, be an experience not dissimilar to lawyers adapting their substantive legal advice and also practice management to the internet and to mobile technologies. Many applications that utilize Blockchain will not be overtly labeled as such. Just like many lawyers (and other people) use AI routinely every day, without realizing it, so most Blockchains will likely be invisible to the user, in the applications that use them. Decisions on whether or not to invest in a particular new platform or application will then focus more on its user-facing features and the value that they deliver, than on whether or not it involves Blockchain technology.

Should lawyers learn to code?

It is important for young lawyers joining a firm to understand that the path to partnership today involves the understanding and use of technology on a scale that is unprecedented. Whether lawyers need to learn to actually code though, to create Blockchains or otherwise, is a different question. Being able to code could be a personal differentiator and at the very least, it would help the lawyer to better understand what software can deliver, and how, and its limitations. For matters requiring complex coding, however, cross-training lawyers to be able to do the coding is probably as sensible as cross-training highly talented software developers to practice law. The best solutions will likely always continue to come from top quality lawyers and technology professionals collaborating closely with each other to produce work product that represents the pinnacle of each of their professional capabilities.

Where Blockchains will likely compete with law firms

It is essential for lawyers to accurately understand where the service that they provide to a client is intermedial in nature, versus where it involves the delivery of real, judgment-based advice. A surprising number of services on which law firms currently rely for revenue, when examined very critically, may prove more intermedial than advisory in nature. It is these kinds of services that are most at risk of disruption by Blockchain applications.

Some services comprise a mix of intermedial and advisory, where the advisory component is relatively standardized and susceptible to replacement by AI tools. In such cases, the lawyers providing such services need to build new competencies, which deliver the more sophisticated and high-value services that are possible when the "standardized" part of the work is delivered cheaply and efficiently, through advanced digital tools.

Some of the areas that will likely be disrupted first will involve the maintenance of registers and inventories, for instance real estate title registers, trademarks, or internet domain names. Automation of actions through smart contracts will considerably simplify the drafting of documentation for many forms of contract across both commercial and corporate M&A. Dispute resolution will likely require different approaches and in all but the most complex and important disputes, the fees that lawyers can earn will likely subside dramatically. In all these cases, scope exists for lost work to be replaced with new, more complex, almost certainly more lucrative work, but learning and retooling skills will be prerequisites.

How will Blockchains affect the fundamental business model of law firms?

The people-leveraged, pyramid-shaped, "Tournament of Lawyers" model[2] emerged in the early 20th century. Over the past century, it has proved a highly successful business model for law firms. To understand why it emerged, why it is now under pressure, and what might replace it, it is useful to rebuild one's understanding of the model from the ground up. The "Tournament of Lawyers" model was triggered by radically disruptive technologies that emerged at the end of the 19th century (primarily the internal combustion engine, distributed electricity, and the telephone and radio). Acting together in dynamic and complex combination, these technologies transformed commerce, industry, and society itself in industrialized economies. Law firms had to bulk up and specialize, to meet a whole raft of new legal needs that emerged. Without the digital technologies of today, the only form of leverage that was available was human leverage. The junior associate and the billable hour were born.

As the 20th century progressed and especially after the commercialization of the internet and the World Wide Web in the 1990s, the people-leveraged model came under pressure. That pressure was relieved to a degree by the dotcom boom of the 1990s, followed by the housing credit boom during the first decade of the 21st century. It returned, with a vengeance, with the onset of the global economic crisis of 2008-09.

As we near the end of the second decade of the 21st century, it seems clear that new technological disruptions similar in scale to those of the late 19th century may be looming. AI, Blockchain, big data, the IOT, advanced wireless networks and perhaps even quantum computing, acting together in similarly dynamic, complex concert, seem poised to again transform commerce, industry, and society itself. If that proves to be so, the legal profession will need to remodel itself on a scale unprecedented in a century if it is to adequately serve the needs of clients and society in the new world that results.

> *"Forecasting is always dangerous, especially about the future."*

Attributed variously to Niels Bohr, Mark Twain, and Yogi Berra, this saying is as true in this case as anywhere else. A cone of uncertainty extends into the future, with the likelihood of forecasts proving accurate decreasing exponentially over time. Even between today and 2025, far too many variables and imponderables exist for one to make forecasts about the future with any hope of certainty. What one can do, however, is draw broad assumptions and create scenarios.

Firms will be more reliant on digital leverage and less on people leverage

Learning from other kinds of professional service firms that have gone through digital transformations, such as architecture and engineering firms, we expect that headcount in firms will reduce while revenues increase.

Pricing models will move from billable hours, to value-based models

When technology is creating substantive value and that value cannot be adequately priced using methods that are incremented in units of human time expended, it is likely that a different model will finally supplant the "billable-hour". Given the strong influence that the "billable-hour" model exerts on the systems, structures, and processes in a modern law firm, this moment is likely to trigger the need for painful business process re-engineering, for firms that have not already begun to transition their business models. (Client demands for higher efficiency and transparency already create an imperative for some of the changes that will then become unavoidable.)

Staffing will depend heavily on professionals at the intersection of technology and law

By 2025, roughly 75 percent of the workforce in developed economies will be "millennials". The oldest will be in their 40s, so a significant percentage of law firm partners and senior leaders will then also be millennials. Barring unforeseen events such as war or plagues, these are simple demographic facts. It follows that over the next seven years, the millennial acceptance of technology will overwhelm the reluctance that older generations have for embracing it. This assumption is as valid in law firms as in their client organizations. On top of that will be the almost certain reality that lawyers will not be able to adequately advise clients on the legal needs that are induced by these same disruptive and transformational digital trends, including Blockchains.

Added to which, it is worth considering what the role of an external legal advisor will be in a world that has become far more complex, and in which up to half of the work currently being sold to clients can be better delivered by technology. Just like in the early 20th century, when the "Tournament of Lawyers" model emerged and small, generalist practices were displaced, lawyers will need to "up their game" and specialize even more deeply. Imagine a world in which a lawyer has at her or his fingertips tools that deliver the work product that has traditionally taken the lion's share of an engagement's time and budget, at little additional cost and almost instantaneously. What opportunities exist in that world for lawyers to deliver a better, more sophisticated, higher value service to clients?

What law firms should be doing now

Become much more conversant with legal implications of Blockchains, for clients

Given the importance of the area generally, it is astonishing that so few lawyers are yet developing practices focused on Blockchains – beyond ICOs, cryptocurrency, and their associated regulatory issues. With low supply and high demand, significant churn exists with such lawyers moving between law firms and establishing their own. Clear needs exist for more lawyers and other professionals who understand both substantive areas of the law and the technical workings of Blockchain protocols, to advise clients on developing and deploying Blockchain-based applications and tools. Needs also exist for intellectual property (IP) lawyers whose practice focuses on Blockchain-induced IP issues. Corporate lawyers are needed who understand the difference between conventional corporations and corporate finance versus decentralized autonomous organizations (DAOs) and the unique legal issues involved with the latter.

While these skills may seem tangential to the main body of client needs at present, this could change quickly. Given the learning curves required, a strategy of "wait and see" may prove risky and the shortage of talent may make hiring it in laterally challenging. Much opportunity apparently exists for lawyers willing and able to retool their skills.

Encourage experimentation within the firm

One should never underestimate the drag effect of inertia. This is especially true with trends that incumbent leaders find unconvincing, threatening, or distasteful. With any radically new technology or other trend, it is usually best to start small and prove the trend with quick, clear successes before attempting major transformational projects. As Blockchain and other digital trends disrupt client legal needs, so the degree to which they threaten lawyers who fail to retool their skills will climb. Finding spaces within the business model where future-focused lawyers can safely experiment and develop solutions early enough for these to be implemented before the pressure to do so becomes inexorable, may prove to be of existential importance to the firm. Finding ways for lawyers to collaborate with technology professionals (such as with Allen & Overy's "Fuse" project, amongst others) is an obvious solution and one that holds the potential to accelerate this learning and development radically. Explorations should focus both on innovations aimed at client legal needs and on enhancing efficiency within the firm.

Clients frequently have as weak a view of their future legal needs as do law firms who advise them. The best way to uncover those emergent needs is through active collaboration between the two. Helping clients better understand their future legal needs that will result from their disruption, including through Blockchain technology, may also be the most significant business development opportunity to have emerged in years, for law firms.

Support clients in being proactive with regulators

Most regulators are themselves going through steep learning curves as they grapple with issues surrounding Blockchains. The possibilities for inappropriate regulation are rife and the risks considerable.

Some law firms have been active in this area for some years already, working with the early pioneers and industry associations dealing with Blockchain issues, advising them on the first subpoenas and law enforcement inquiries, and even keeping their leaders out of jail.

In conclusion

It is clear that the business models of law firms are poised for radical disruption. The areas of law in which a model premised on "billable hours" delivers the best result is reducing steadily. Given the diversity of services and service delivery modalities that is emerging, it is highly likely that the law firms of the future will adopt multiple business models, to extract optimum performance. Perhaps even multiple brands. Legal process outsourcing businesses, the "Big Four" global advisory/accounting firms, and other non-traditional legal service providers with different business models believe that the future belongs to them. To remain relevant, law firms need to discover how to undergo the digital transformation required while maintaining current performance, and prove them wrong.

This chapter originally appeared in *Blockchain and the Legal Profession*, published in July 2018.

References

1. Opening speech at the Fourth Cash Symposium of the Deutsche Bundesbank, Frankfurt am Main, 14 February 2018, accessed at www.bundesbank.de/Redaktion/EN/Reden/2018/2018_02_14_weidmann.html
2. So-called because of the first book written to describe it, namely: Galanter, M. and Palay, T. (1991) *Tournament of Lawyers: The Transformation of the Big Law Firm*. University of Chicago Press.

Part two:
People and culture

Chapter 4: Flexible working arrangements – the next stage from the "office nine-to-five"

By Dr Bailey Bosch, director of people and culture, and Katherine Thomas, CEO, FreeRange Lawyers

We live in extraordinary times, where the use of digital communication technology has turned the world of work on its head and has totally redefined what it means to "go to work". Work is now no longer a place. It is often not a time. Increasingly, work is simply the sum of a series of producing tasks that can be undertaken "any time, any place, anywhere" (the "Martini" approach).

So far, so good. In fact, this may sound like work utopia to many. The opportunity to control one's day – how one works – is the goal of many women (and men). However, in this chapter, we argue that current practices in the legal profession still have a long way to go to embrace the "Martini" philosophy of work and that, in many cases, the tension between possibility and reality causes considerable frustration amongst lawyers looking for a smarter and more humane way to operate. Furthermore, it is possible to argue that unique demands usually placed on women mean that lack of genuine flexibility inhibits women's ability to progress in their careers. The latest England and Wales Law Society's Annual Statistics Report released in September 2018[1] shows that although 50.1 percent of all lawyers in the jurisdiction are female, only 29 percent of all partners are women. What is happening to the other 21 percent? Why do we still not see anywhere near equal representation of men and women in the profession's most senior ranks?

We propose that in order for women to advance their careers in the legal sector, more law companies need to embrace a change in working practices to allow for an individual to work flexibly and remotely, where possible. We advocate for a radical shift in thinking that does away with traditional methods of surveillance (like billable hours and the jacket on the chair) towards a culture of trust and the recognition of individual agency and accountability. Allowing individuals choice over when and where they do their work offers enormous benefits to the individual. At the same time, it provides significant commercial advantage too.

"Flexible work", "work/life balance", and "wellbeing" are common topics of discussion in social media and industry publications, where well-intentioned sentiment often replaces evidence as the mainstay of discussion. In this chapter, we take a different approach. Using evidence to support our assertions, we define flexible work and then remind ourselves that it hasn't always been this way, with a brief look at how we arrived at our current office practices. We then look at flexible working arrangements and why they are still seen as primarily a women's issue. Lastly, we go on to outline the benefits of flexible working for businesses and conclude by suggesting alternative ways in which women can discuss, form, and negotiate flexible work within their own careers.

What is flexible work?

A note on terminology: flexible work is not the same as, but is closely linked to, agile working, which the author defined for the legal profession in a 2016 update as:

> *"...starting with the client and focusing on achieving outputs rather than managing inputs. It encompasses every area of the organization and matches resources of all types to meet demands efficiently and adapt to changing market conditions nimbly. Crucially, agile working in legal services exists where business needs overlap with worker preferences and skills, resulting in increased productivity, efficiency, adaptability and innovation."*[2]

FT.com's lexicon[3] defines flexible working as "giving employees flexibility on how long, where and when they work". This can take many forms, but, according to Lucy Dickens of "The Juggle",[4] usually falls into one or more of five categories:

- Adjusted hours – having different working hours from the company's standard operating hours;
- Flexi time – choosing start and finish times but working during core hours;
- Compressed weeks – longer hours over fewer days;
- Job sharing – two people sharing one job and splitting the hours; and
- Remote working – working away from the office.

In practice, rights to request flexible working vary from one country to another. In Australia, for example, the Fair Work Act in 2010 gave workers the right to request flexible working if they fulfilled certain criteria, such as being a carer or having a disability. The UK went further in 2014 with The Children and Families Act, which gives anyone the right to request flexible working, regardless of their demographic or out of work responsibilities.

In both cases, however, since the right is only to *request* flexible work, the existence of FWA policies does not guarantee an employee access to flexible work arrangements and often the implementation of the policy is at the discretion of an employee's immediate supervisor who generally has the authority to approve, decline, encourage, or discourage their use. In practice then, many flexible work arrangements are not formalized employment agreements but rather informal ad hoc arrangements between the employee and their supervisor.[5] This means that for an employee to take up a flexible working arrangement they need the explicit support of their supervisor.

Work hasn't always been this way

It is human nature to assume that the way things are now are the way that they have always been. Similarly, it is human nature to assume that our current state is the culmination of previous generations' mistakes that enabled us to arrive at this final stage, this pinnacle of achievement. Of course, when we think rationally, we know neither to be true, but it doesn't stop us being subconsciously influenced by these notions.

So, let's challenge those perceptions. "Work" through the ages has comprised a wide variety of activities and situations, from laboring on the family farm, to itinerant merchants, to medieval monks writing in quiet spaces specifically designed for copying and creating manuscripts. It was only in the 18th century, with the advent of large-scale factories that the notion of work as a place with fixed – and monitored – times, became more established. Until then, work happened when and where it needed to happen.

Why is this relevant to a discussion around flexible working? Well, flexible working is still seen as an alternative to the "norm" of nine-to-five, in-office work, and any discussion of flexible working therefore necessarily entails a justification of why we should break from this norm. Look at things through an historical lens, however, and it becomes easier to see flexible working as the next stage of working practice that simply supersedes the "office nine-to-five". Sometimes, it helps to look back before looking forward.

Why is flexible working seen as primarily a woman's issue?

It is understandable that the issue of workplace flexibility is still largely seen as a "woman's issue" as working time arrangements have different impacts on men and women.[6]

Heywood and Miller's research[7] evidences what many of us know to be true – that women experience greater levels of negative spill-over between job and family life than men. This informs a woman's decision to take and hold jobs characterized by demanding and/or uncertain work schedules. Add into the mix the fact that, as the OECD Statistics in 2016 told us, women are more likely to work on a part-time basis than men and that organizational cultures tend to reinforce gender roles and it becomes easier to see why there is such a disparity between the number of women entering the legal profession and the number occupying senior roles.

The ideal worker is seen as someone who is able to give priority to work with no outside distractions. Historically, this has been a male worker with a female partner at home who takes care of the domestic duties, allowing him to dedicate himself to his work. Some argue that the norm of the ideal worker is less relevant nowadays as women's participation in the workforce approaches that of men's, but there is plenty of evidence[8] for its continued existence.

However, if we are to move the discussion around flexible working forward, we need to stop pigeon-holing this as a woman's issue or, worse still, a Mum's issue. In doing so, we fall into the trap of assuming all women experience life in the same way and that there is a common experience of motherhood (and, conversely, a common experience of manhood). We know that is just not the case. Individuals differ. Family structures differ. The children themselves differ. To lump all experiences into one homogenous category loses the richness that comes from individual difference. To do so ignores the essence of what flexible work is all about – the tailoring of an employee's working life to meet their individual needs. Flexible working arrangements are relevant to all employees and an organization that makes them available to all who are suitable is going to create a workplace that promotes equity and equality.

The organizational benefits of flexible work

Job satisfaction

One of the most commonly researched outcomes of flexible working arrangements is job satisfaction, which is defined as an employee's affective or emotional reaction to a job based on comparing actual outcomes with desired outcomes.[9] Overall, FWAs have been positively related to the job satisfaction of employees. If an organization can increase job satisfaction amongst its staff it will benefit by increasing organizational commitment, reducing staff turnover, reducing human resource costs, increasing productivity, and by the creation of brand ambassadors. In this way, the use of FWAs as a mechanism to improve job satisfaction provides tangible gains for a business.

Productivity

The concept of productivity refers to the employee's capacity to generate products or services needed to achieve organization goals. High work productivity improves organizational performance and this is why organizations seek the best ways to enhance employee productivity to generate sustainable and positive impacts. Looking at it from an economic employer-focused perspective, most organizations think in terms of numbers of hours per day they can get from (and compensate for) a worker. We suggest a shift towards a productivity model may be better suited to work that entails FWAs. Research literature on teleworking[10] suggests that managers deal with the challenge of not being able to monitor the actions of teleworkers by placing more emphasis on output controls. A greater emphasis on outcomes causes a lesser emphasis on inputs. Suddenly the hours worked, when they are worked, and where they are worked, pale into insignificance when the only measurement is output produced.

Attracting and retaining talent

Flexibility is a business imperative for companies who want to retain and attract a diverse talent pool. There are currently four generations amongst the working population – the traditionalists, Baby Boomers, Generation X and Generation Y (also known as Millennials). Millennials are the digital natives amongst the working population, the ones who are looking for different ways to work and embrace the use of technology to allow work to be done anywhere and at any time. Organizations that fail to offer Millennials their expected working environment run the risk of failing to attract highly qualified, intelligent, and productive employees. A recent international survey found that 89 percent of working people thought that flexible working should become normal.[11] This generation also cares about sustainability and removing the need for real estate and commuting sends a signal to this talent pool that an organization is forward-thinking and environmentally aware.

Cost efficiency

Offices were originally designed with cubicles (what are referred to as cellular-type office arrangements) but during the 1950s open-plan designs were introduced and gained popularity during the 1970s due to their space-saving efficiency. An open-plan office design eliminates dividing walls and therefore requires less space. The cost of office space is approximately $20,000 per workstation per annum in London and Hong Kong and even in developing countries with rapid-growth economies such as Indonesia, workstations cost between $2,000 per year in Surabaya and up to $5,000 per year in Jakarta. Since 2009, prime location rental costs in the City of London have increased by 68 percent and in mid-town London this figure is even higher at 88 percent.

In order to further save money, companies have opted for flexi-desking or desk-sharing concepts where employees are not allocated individual desks but rather share with others. Over 70 percent of European and American firms apply open-desk or flexi-desk options allowing companies such as IBM to save up to $100m annually by using this option in its US and European offices.

However, with an open-plan design it is no surprise that employees report an increase in distraction. While the open-plan space cuts costs for the company, employees report noise, distraction, and lack of privacy as being problematic in such settings, and there is evidence to suggest open-plan offices reduce employees' attention, productivity, creativity and satisfaction.[12]

Satisfaction with the physical environment is related to work satisfaction and productivity, and privacy is positively related to work productivity. Organizations that allow their employees to work from home can mitigate the risk of distraction caused by an open-plan office and can save money by eliminating the need for office space at all in some cases. Of course, there are going to be distractions for an employee who works from home as well, but the key difference is the home is a domain where the employee has control and autonomy. Noisy environment? Eliminate the source or move to a different room. Find you work better with fresh air? Open all the windows and don't worry about having to consider anyone else's preferences. With some planning and the deliberate use of strategies, common worries an organization might have about allowing their staff to work from home can be eliminated. Never underestimate the power of giving an individual autonomy over their activity – you will likely find they will exceed expectations. From an organization's point of view, office space is costly, and allowing FWAs whereby individuals can choose to work from home eliminates the need for a desk. A reduced physical footprint also saves on the cost of practical office-keeping needs.

When you add into the discussion the daily show-up rate, it makes further commercial sense to have people working from home. The average daily show-up rate of partners and associates in law firms is between 70 and 80 percent, which means that office utilization is on average between 55 and 65 percent,[13] when taking into account those out of the office due to business trips, client meetings, secondments, and leave. Adopting flexible working policies allows organizations to save money on redundant office space and signals to potential employees that they care about sustainability.

Diversity

One of the major benefits FWAs offer organizations is their role in increasing diversity.

Diversity has to mean more than just ensuring that the images used in a company's branding tick all of the 'options' boxes. Men? Check. Women? Check. People of color? Check. Differently-abled? Um... not yet. Gender fluid? Hang on, will check Shutterstock for a suitable photo. Striving for true diversity needs to be more than just a public relations exercise. Giving options to ALL people to engage in meaningful employment changes lives and when we change lives, we can change families, and so on the ripple effect rides. In order to appreciate true diversity, we need to extend our understanding beyond the stereotypical collection of diverse "groups". We need to think beyond set quotas to ensure gender or ethnic equality, for example. In order to be a truly diverse workplace, organizations need to think outside of the confines of "minority" groups and recognize that in fact, every worker is their own unique and wonderful collection of "diversities" that collectively contribute to the wider culture of the organization.

Within the constraints of the organization's compulsory business activity, we should be looking at how work can be structured to achieve true flexibility for those engaging in it. Is there a compelling reason why Stanley in Accounts can't do his routine work activities that aren't time sensitive at 3am when he naturally wakes and doesn't go back to sleep? Why can't Mandi in policy finish off her document reviews after her evening yoga class when her mind feels clear and alert? Will there be any real problems caused by Michael coming in to work at 10am after he has taken his youngest child to kindergarten? Why are we forcing Lorraine to navigate public transport and walk from the station to her desk in the office when her joints are burning with arthritis? A truly flexible work policy will meet each employee where they are and scaffold around their individual needs. It will not force the company's interpretation of what flexibility means on to the employee, but rather will empower the employee to craft a working day that truly reflects how they want, and need, to structure their time and availability and ultimately how they want to live their life.

Offering flexible work options allows an organization to increase diversity and in this global marketplace, diversity is a currency that can provide a competitive edge.

Forming flexible working arrangements

Here's our alternative take on how to approach working flexibly.

First, take a long, hard look at your current situation and where you would like it to be. Articulate that future state to yourself by writing it down. Be specific – for example, instead of "more time at home", say "I'd like to be back home by 5pm every day to have dinner with my family".

Second, identify the elements that can be achieved through working flexibly and be clear about those that can't. It's likely that some of your ideal future state has nothing to do with working arrangements and it's best to be clear about that upfront. Flexible working doesn't solve everything.

Next, formulate an approach to work that will meet your plans. Be specific. Be realistic. Be honest with yourself.

Now is the time to present your case at work. Prepare a short, written document that outlines your request – specifically – and, if necessary, explains why you would like to work in this way. Make a balanced case, so avoid being preachy about the benefits of flexible work. Instead, use specific examples of success, either with colleagues or other companies that have adopted similar approaches to yours. Be upfront about the potential challenges of your working arrangement for the company, for your colleagues, and for you. Clearly identify ways to address them.

Once you're working flexibly, play your part to make it a success. Yes, this will likely mean give and take on both sides at times, but it will also require new habits and new discipline from you to set boundaries and parameters within your day. Don't be one of the flexible workers who doesn't experience the benefit because they can't shake off old habits.

Actively plan to take care of yourself – both physically and mentally. In a recent Thrive Global article,[14] the author suggested that to avoid burnout (which is a potential risk for those working remotely) you should change your expectations to better align with your current circumstances. Yes, you might miss out on some of the office goings-on because you are not there physically but if you expect that, it won't hit you as rejection or loss. Think carefully about how your new way of working will look, and adjust your expectations accordingly. You might need to more actively explore ways you can connect with others so that you avoid isolation and maintain your relationships with colleagues.

Support others to work flexibly – not just women or carers. The more we all do to normalize flexible working as an issue for everyone, the more likely it is to become the next stage in the evolution of work following on from the "office nine-to-five".

Summary

Flexible working arrangements are relevant to all employees and should not be limited to just one sub-group of the working population. Not only do these arrangements allow individuals an opportunity to develop and nurture a life outside of their careers but they are a powerful business tool that can be leveraged to increase productivity, diversity, and sustainability.

This chapter originally appeared in *Career Development for Women Lawyers*, published in March 2019.

References

1. https://www.lawsociety.org.uk/support-services/research-trends/annual-statistics-report-2017/
2. https://remakinglawfirms.com/agile-working-and-the-legal-sector-towards-a-clearer-definition/
3. http://lexicon.ft.com/Term?term=flexible-working
4. https://www.lucydickens.com.au/the-juggle-podcast/
5. McNamara, T. K., Pitt-Catsouphes, M., Brown, M., & Matz-Costa, C. (2012). "Access to and utilization of flexible work options." *Industrial Relations*, 51(4), 936–964.
6. Uglanova, E., and Dettmers, J. (2018). "Sustained Effects of Flexible Working Time Arrangements on Subjective Well-Being." *Journal of Happiness Studies, 19*(6), 1727-1748.
7. Heywood, J. S., & Miller, L. (2014). *Schedule flexibility, family friendly policies and absence.* The Manchester School, 83(6), 652–675.
8. Pocock, B. (2005a). "Work–life 'balance' in Australia: Limited progress, dim prospects." *Asia Pacific Journal of Human Resources*, 43, 198–209.
9. Lyness, K. S., Gornick, J.S. Stone, P., and Grotto, A.R. (2012). "It's All about Control: Worker Control Over Schedule and Hours in Cross-National Context." *American Sociological Review*, 77, 1023–49.
10. Felstead, A., Jewson, N., and Walters, S. (2003). Managerial control of employees working at home. *British Journal of Industrial Relations, 41*, 241–264.

11. https://www.hcamag.com/au/news/general/flexible-work-is-the-new-normal-survey/152294#.Wu-qp2lpwXo.linkedin
12. https://slate.com/business/2016/05/open-plan-offices-add-distractions-and-hurt-productivity.html
13. CBRE Law Firm Practice Group, Law in London 2016. *The Changing Law Office*. September 2016.
14. https://thriveglobal.com/stories/the-positive-power-of-stress/

Chapter 5: Modern career trajectories – is partnership still the end goal?

By Clare Harman Clark, senior professional support lawyer, Taylor Wessing

There is a great story about the UK's first women lawyers. In 1922, having passed the Law Society's final exams with flying colors, Carrie Morrison, Maud Crofts, Mary Pickup, and Mary Sykes were convinced to race along the Chancery Lane cobbles, skirts flying, in a bid to be the first admitted to the rolls. If this seems unlikely, it was against all odds that they had even made it this far. Gwyneth Bebb had taken the Law Society to the Court of Appeal back in 1913 only to be told that women could not be lawyers as they did not qualify as "persons" under the Solicitors Act of 1843; it took the Sex Disqualification Act of 1919 before the Law Society was forced to concede its manly stronghold on the profession and let the ladies in. As it happened, Morrison hammered on the Law Society door first (or, just perhaps, she finished her articles before the others), and became officially the first woman solicitor in England and Wales. But while the dash along the cobbles was not the first uphill schlep for women within the legal profession, it also wasn't to be the last; for many the race is not yet won.

Women might have secured industry participation, but generations of lawyers have come and gone and there remains stubborn inequality among the highest ranks of the profession. The partnership path is arduous but is it really still weighted against women? Do they just *want* it less? Is partnership still the end goal for lawyers joining the profession in any case? For the best part of a century, many believe that the practice of law has failed to find a way of accommodating its female foot soldiers. Lawyers entering the industry today have arguably more options than ever to tread a career trajectory that doesn't end in traditional partnership, but how realistic is it that they will find, and follow, these new paths?

The path to partner

There is very little sprinting to be done along the traditional career path for your average lawyer, male or female. Partnership is a statutory entity devised in the 19th century and, notwithstanding the changes to liability at the turn of the millennium, most law firms have maintained a formal hierarchy. Their triangular fee-earning structures start with trainees at the bottom and rising (reducing) ranks of associate until the apex, when promotion to partner is an invitation largely made depending on market conditions, business case, and experience. Many firms have also introduced a salaried partner role, which offers a business card for the ambitious without a stake in equity (or the larger slabs of remuneration).

If joining the partnership is still the presumed career goal of most junior solicitors, the attrition point is an important one. There is not so much space at the top. As one respondent to ARK's recent research on the topic (which is examined further below eloquently explained, "Attrition is necessary for success in the status quo".

Research published in *The Lawyer* in 2016[1] suggests that the coveted title is conferred in top London firms at somewhere between nine and 13 years' post qualification experience (PQE). For everyone else, it may well be a case of up or out. In practice, the effect of this statistic results in a dramatic gender imbalance as the rump of solicitors left in private practice by the time they reach nine years' PQE, during which time families are embarked on and lives built, tends to be male. Unsurprisingly then, according to SRA figures, in 2017, 71 percent of partners in the largest law firms (those with 50 plus partners) are men.[2] This statistic alone suggests that the industry's career path rigidity is not working for everyone.

The lay of the land

In January 2019, ARK Group undertook some interesting primary research amongst its global subscribers. Responses were gathered at all levels of the legal profession, with job titles ranging from legal assistant through to managing partner. Asked *"Do you agree that modern career trajectories have changed, and partnership is no longer the end goal?"* the outcome was surprisingly stark. On the simple collection of yes and no answers, a total of 63 percent thought that partnership is no longer the end goal, compared to only 31 percent who thought it was. That leaves just six percent unsure.

It is interesting to explore in more granularity the stories behind the percentages. The survey welcomed additional thoughts and, of those who responded more fully, a slightly higher 67 percent then thought that partnership is, most likely, no longer the end goal, despite that "common sense says that should be the case". Of course, various commentators thought their colleagues are still committed to the traditional ladder.

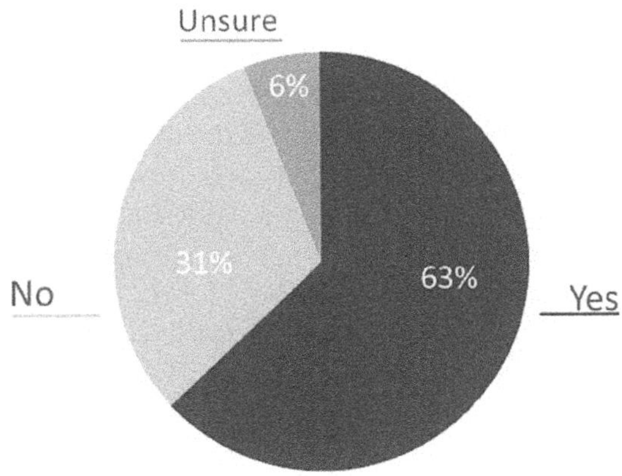

Figure 1: Do you agree that modern career trajectories have changed, and partnership is no longer the end goal?

The third of respondents in this category made comments that ranged from the confident assertion that "every attorney, male or female, in a law firm wants [partnership]," through to the slightly more circumspect "partnership is still the goal for most professional women". None of these answers elucidated the benefits of a partner job title, however. Perhaps these are obvious, too widely understood to warrant explanation, but it is interesting that the respondents in the 67 percent group were far more forthcoming with their experiences.

For most, an ambivalence to the aspiration of partnership came down to the fact that attaining the coveted role was simply too hard, "so unattainable" or even "not realistic" in a large firm. The rules around qualifying for partnership status were often found to be frustratingly opaque. In past decades, commentators believed that "partnership was forced upon associates". The likelihood now, however, is that the ambitious associate will be asked to provide a detailed business case in order to justify promotion, something "much less so the case 20 years ago". This is not such a welcome development: "it is intentionally nebulous and difficult to qualify, and it is used to excuse law firms from promoting attorneys to partnership". For what is supposed to be an aspirational goal, this perception doesn't encourage confidence.

Of course, much reference was also made to the life-changing (and impliedly life-limiting) consequences of "all the required commitments". It's a pie-eating competition where the prize is more pie. One respondent reported taking an of counsel role in preference to a partnership position "because of the flexibility that it affords me". What exactly constitutes *too much to ask* of a partner in terms of hours, responsibility or liability often seemed to come down to a generational shift. "Millennials' attitudes are very different on this," said one interviewee. Another concluded simply, "Entitled millennials [...] expect a life/work balance". The point was echoed elsewhere (albeit with less latent irritation): "I have seen a shift with the millennials wanting more of a work–life balance rather than just partnership." Gendered perceptions aside, many younger lawyers today simply feel that the role is "not all that it is cracked up to be".

This certainly accords with general, broad-brush understanding of millennial trends; however, maybe it is also because the cost benefit analysis of partnership commitment does not warrant promotion, particularly to those diluted *salaried* partner positions. "The financial rewards are not what they once were, and the sacrifices too great," said one respondent. Also, many of the associates now at sufficient PQE to be considering partnership witnessed first-hand the effects of the 2008 global recession, riding the wave of a brand-new career through the front door as more senior lawyers were carried out the back under riptides of redundancy. The years' worth of sacrifices demanded by progression might not be worth it when you think that you might also end up in any event a casualty of the external economic environment.

Interestingly, it is worth noting that none of the answers given made explicit reference to gender. To consider the elephant in the room, a key to addressing historic imbalance involves recognizing that family life often requires a facilitator. A large part of the reason for such imbalance at the upper echelons of the workplace is because, traditionally, that facilitating role has been taken on by the wife and mother (in the absence of a paid housekeeper or nanny). A Law Society survey in 2018 reported that an astonishing 91 percent of people recognize that flexible working arrangements are critical to improving diversity. Serious work is now underway in many firms to readdress the gender balance at partnership level, and a lot of this involves offering flexible working arrangements that didn't exist a decade ago.

Of the 100 respondents to the survey, only six were male. Perhaps this is understandable, given the subject area; perhaps not. Of the male respondents, 60 percent defended the importance of partnership. It is perhaps interesting that no one mentioned a lack of female role models in many current partnerships, or powerful female business mentors generally, but also no commentator mentioned feeling or witnessing disenchantment with law as a career per se. Yet for all the reasons discussed above still "many decide along the way that partnership is not for them".

The problem may well be a structural one, leading us back to the point made earlier about the inflexibility of law firms generally when it comes to creating other aspirational career paths. Many complained that "law firms have not come up with viable alternatives". There are occasionally upper level alternatives, such as consultant, of counsel, legal director or managing associate. These were generally introduced with the express purpose of stemming senior associate attrition, but there is no standardization of these roles in the industry, and little real agreement on what the new job titles mean; depending on the firm they might constitute another stepping stone to partnership or an attempt to offer a viable, visible alternative. Ultimately, however, many respondents felt that partnership dilutions were not as appealing as they had hoped. "The management or the model [of law firms] is not yet fully up to speed," when they offer "second best" alternatives. In this failure, many women are looking for other answers and as one respondent warned, young lawyers "will vote with their feet and leave for more interesting career options if their firm doesn't offer them".

A bridge to brave new worlds

Arguably, for the first time since that race on Chancery Lane began, the rules of the race are being set by the runners. One important generational shift has been that careers need no longer exist in professional silos, and it is hard to overestimate the transferable skillsets demanded by legal training. At the higher operational levels, being a lawyer takes an ability to draft, present, and persuade. It demands the confidence of a subject matter expert, the efficiency of a project manager, and high levels of commercial acumen and financial awareness, in a bid to solve today's problems while effectively anticipating tomorrow's. It is easy to see how a stint in private practice can easily facilitate a move in-house or towards government. Depending on subject experience, the skills lend themselves to many entirely different career paths.

Within law firms themselves, there are trailblazers in the knowledge management field. For many years, an application for the job of professional support lawyer was the only path available to associates more interested in (black letter law and) work–life balance. When the role was first developed in the 1990s London market, part-time working was virtually non-existent; little surprise perhaps so many PSLs across the country are women (often with assumed caring responsibility for children). For decades, the role was arguably perceived as a back-office option for those unwilling to leave private practice but not quite ambitious enough to lead it. It has always been a respected role, but often one seen as fundamentally unchallenging to the way the business of a law firm continues.

This is changing dramatically with the professionalization of KM standards (ISO 30401:2018) and the sharp elbows of PSLs redefining their careers as bridges between business development and legal practice. It's vital work at all levels of the industry. It clearly goes to the heart of the high-cost, high-reputation players, but for firms focused on commoditized work, staring down the barrel at blockchain efficiencies, it is more important now than ever to identify, articulate, and promote value-add in terms of (human) legal excellence. Knowledge is the greatest commodity of a law firm, and the industry is starting, slowly, to offer an alternative career path that reflects this. There are increasing numbers of appointments of board level positions for KM practitioners. It's partnership, of a kind, just not as we know it.

While the structural ladders of law firm progression are taking a while to dismantle from the top, legal technology is busy building a brave new world from the bottom up. Best placed to understand the limitations and ministrations of practicing life in a law firm, and to spot the possibilities for transactional efficiency, entrepreneurial associates are bridging the professional gap between practice and tech, carving out brand new and exciting roles in innovation. This leap is made possible by advancements in machine learning and AI processes, and facilitated by firms interested in capturing diverse ideas, not just diverse gender balance.

Where the creativity of these associates is not harnessed within their firms, they are jumping ship entirely to run start-ups, selling products back to the legal market and challenging gender stereotypes in the science, technology, engineering, and mathematics (STEM) world while they are at it. At cutting edge firms across the world such as Luminescence, or Automio, or Tessian, there are women whose ambition has seen them leap to the other side of the table. Rather than managing legal practice from the inside, these trained lawyers are literally redefining it from the out.

Conclusion

In 2017, the Law Society Annual Report revealed that overall, a (slim) majority of practicing solicitors were now women. It's an upwards trend – women made up a record 61.6 percent share of those freshly admitted to the Roll.[3] Morrison would be proud. It has taken the best part of a century but slowly, and surely, at the lower rungs at least, we have gone from tolerated participation to industry majority. On these figures alone, the idea that future generations will still ponder at a partnership gender imbalance seems ridiculous. Yet from a law firm perspective, considering the results of ARK's recent research, the question of inspiring those women to climb the traditional ladder is less about some lip-service follow-through to diversity pledges, and more one of continued relevance in reflecting the clients they work for. It's about finding a way to flourish, not simply survive. Because until the partner role is reinstated as an achievable and aspirational goal, the most talented might just throw the race, and run towards a growing number of exciting professional, challenging, and innovative alternatives.

This chapter originally appeared in *Career Development for Women Lawyers*, published in March 2019.

References

1. www.thelawyer.com/making-partner-firms-shorten-route/
2. www.sra.org.uk/solicitors/diversity-toolkit/diverse-law-firms.page
3. www.lawsociety.org.uk/support-services/research-trends/annual-statistics-report-2017/

Chapter 6: The law department of the future – What will good look like?

By Janvi Patel, VP, Elevate and chairwoman, Halebury

Historically, when we think of law departments, we have a vision of departments within traditional law firms. However, due to the unbundling of legal services, many different and unique legal service providers have established, and each of those essentially has its own law department.

Building a resilient law department for the future will be very different according to whether you are a General Counsel, the managing partner of a traditional law firm, or the CEO of a NewLaw firm or an alternative legal services provider. Our profession and market space has changed significantly over the last 10 years and it continues to do so. In line with this rapid pace of change, it is safe to say that law departments will look completely different in the future.

When looking at a law department, I take a simplistic view on areas to consider – people or infrastructure, or as Bjarne Tellmann in *Building an Outstanding Legal Team so* eloquently puts it, the "software or hardware".[1]

This chapter will focus on five key areas; skills, creating the right culture, succession planning, the future of work, and technology. Clearly there is a lot more to a law department of the future than those five areas, such as risk management and alignment of clients and services to name but a few. However, I firmly believe that the base of any legal or law department is its team and infrastructure and this chapter therefore focuses on those themes.

Skills

We are still very much a profession that depends on the skills of lawyers. Although technology might change what we do and how we do it, legal teams still need to focus on people and their skills.

Skills may be different according to which kind of law department someone works in. For our flexible resourcing team at Elevate, our lawyers need to have the ability to hit the ground running, understand legal and commercials in a certain way and understand risk and the industry. That is because we provide flexible resourcing solutions for in-house legal teams. This often means that our team have 24 hours' notice to run a major transaction. It is not necessarily the same skill set that is required for a junior lawyer, property, personal injury or infrastructure lawyer.

The profession is exceptionally broad and the skill sets required are varied in line with this. It goes without saying that a basic understanding of the law is essential in any legal role, but what we require from members of any legal department is much wider than the pure theory, than writing, communication and analytical skills. To ensure lawyers are ready for the future it means the following.

Understanding business

This means from every angle; the operational side, the financial side, the talent side – what business you are in and, in the case of external providers, what business your client is in. On the financials, any lawyer working within a law department, whether in-house or in private practice, needs to know how to create and play with excel spreadsheets. If you want to be fully integrated with your commercial team as well as a project manager (see below), you will need this tool and also the ability to understand it.

How to manage a project

Legal project management (LPM) is a growing skill set and an increasingly important one. However, LPM within traditional law firms is distinctly different from LPM within in-house teams. In traditional law firms, LPM usually means project managing matters to ensure that they are resourced appropriately and in line with client budgets and requirements. For in-house legal teams, LPM means project managing the transaction or project, which usually involves aspects such as working with commercial teams, managing the risk of the transaction, and working with the legal team on implementation/termination or project launch.

Understanding the business of law

This seems straightforward and we usually take this as a given, but I was six years' PQE when I first realized how traditional law firm targets are set, what percentage of the target my salary represented, and how the law firm's finances operate. It is essential, whether you work in-house, for a traditional law firm, an LPO, or an alternative legal service provider, that you understand the business of your legal department. Remember it is hard to support and service a business unless you fully understand it.

EQ, EQ, EQ

I cannot stress how important emotional quotient is. If you have the right EQ, you will have an engaged audience, real buy in, and a seat at the table. It forms the basis of a client/professional relationship. EQ is not easy to teach, but it is teachable. A great way to do this is by helping people "get out of their box", so that they widen their horizons and their networks, both culturally as well as socially. Encouraging NED positions, mentoring the next generation, and coaching people from different social and economic backgrounds, or working with mentoring organizations, can be a real benefit to assist with EQ development, and also with helping lawyers get out of their silos and understand business.

Creating the right culture

Creating the right culture within a legal department is not just about how an individual relates to their client base, but how the legal team work with each other, the environment of a legal department, and also the values that are at the core of that department. Culture is central and vital to building the law department of tomorrow.

A large part of my job involves recruitment, and I can usually tell apart different private practice lawyers via the firms they trained. However, it is hard to tell in-house lawyers apart. This is usually because in-house legal departments tend to be less focused on creating the right culture within their legal department, rather depending on the culture of the company to achieve this. It is important that any in-house team's culture is aligned to the culture of the company, but it must also have its own identity.

To determine what your culture should be, start with understanding what your law department is striving to be. What does good look like to your law department? Understanding the long-term vision of the law department and its ethos is essential to create culture.

I would also suggest taking this to the next level and thinking beyond the law department to the supply chain. If you are working in-house, ensure that your external counsel – be they traditional law firms, NewLaw providers, LPOs and any other providers – are aligned to your law department's culture.

Succession planning

Succession planning is key to any business and any department. At Elevate, we think about it all the time; from the impact it will have on revenue flow to the operational impact, succession planning is essential. I recall one of my supervising partners in my early career saying, "Always think about what would happen to your matters if you got hit by a bus". The comment has stuck with me ever since. However, succession planning should not just be about managing matters but also about having a stable workforce.

If your law department operational structure is a pyramid, consider what it means for your team, especially for the junior members who might not make it to the top of the pyramid. In traditional law firms, the pyramid structure has worked well for succession planning because it enables career progression in terms of position and remuneration. For in-house law departments that tend to have a very flat pyramid structure and no equity track, career progression and therefore succession planning needs to be carefully examined.

At Elevate, we have a flat structure for our legal team who are all senior in-house lawyers who range from paralegals to senior lawyers to legal operations professionals. This means that we have had to look at career development succession planning in another way. We have career management tools that enable use to focus on each team member's career goals and it is what we review regularly. This plan ensures that the team and the business are aligned and that career goals are being met. Other organizations create career progression and opportunity by giving team members the chance to move around other departments or work as project managers for a period of time. Without proper succession planning, any law department team will lack long-term stability.

The future of work

There has been a lot written about the future of work, with regard to both the legal profession specifically and the wider business world. As a profession, we have been late to the table when it comes to flexibility and agile working, but we are picking up pace. Recently, firms such as Baker McKenzie and others have offered flexible working or agile working to all staff. This is a big step.

When building the law department of the future, we have to understand the employment market and its needs. Flexible/agile working takes into account the 24/7 global economy we work in, the commute times and costs, the requirements of a working family, as well as the fact that the best teams are not one-dimensional.

For agile/flexible working to work effectively, the legal department needs to ensure that it is properly resourced, and that might mean with external flexible resource. It is critical that any law department of the future not only adopts, but believes in and genuinely advocates, agile working practices.

Technology

Over the last 10 years there has been an incredible amount of investment in legal technology, both by traditional law firms as well as other providers. I have seen some fascinating platforms and analytics around legal technology. When Elevate was founded in 2011, there were only a couple of document management systems which were cloud based. We have clearly come a long way.

Most leaders of law departments know that technology has to play a key part in the department's future, not just because it makes sense, but also because risk management and cost management is becoming too big without a centralized, automated system.

When thinking about technology, I like to simplify the process into three key areas:

1. Risk/compliance management – document management and content management systems, some of which can assist with project management and risk management. Risk management and contract management is a key area of concern for in-house law departments who see themselves as the "guardians of risk".
2. Automation – which deals with creating and analyzing documentation. The efficiency automation can create has been well-documented; however, any system is only as good as the data, and therefore as good as the user. More information on this point follows below.
3. Project management tools that help increase efficiency and effectiveness of projects and matters.

There are interesting tools for all three areas, but what is essential for tech are the following:

- Implementation – the implementation process sounds straightforward, but anyone who has worked with a legal department or as a technology provider will tell you it is anything but. However, it is fundamental. By "the implementation process", I mean the full process, starting from the scoping exercise, pre-implementation preparation to the actual implementation/launch and for a period of time beyond. Preparation, preparation, preparation;
- Data analysis – Bill Gates' book, *Business @ the Speed of Thought*[2] is fascinating. It helps us to understand how having access to the right data and therefore information can fundamentally change the

game. Obtaining information from any technology programme is key – do not limit it to legal spend but also efficiency of deal flow and risk management. It will enable heads of legal departments to make informed decisions on real data. It is what we lawyers call "proof" and it is what business needs to make a real and meaningful impact; and

- Change management – you can spend millions on tech, from the procurement process to implementation, but any technology is only as good as the data inputted. This means that any tech implementation must have real engagement and buy in from your team, which means you will need some form of change management programme. We have to remember that nobody likes change, and that definitely applies to busy law departments.

The above three points will also help you to reassess the culture of the team and make sure that any tech implementation is aligned to your vision and that of the company.

The law department of tomorrow, whether in private practice, in-house or otherwise, will for many have a different operational structure than the traditional law firm pyramid structure. I have discussed these within my chapter in *New Directions in Legal Services.*[3] To build such a department, I would strongly suggest that you start by asking yourself "What does good look like?" with respect to each of the five points above. The legal profession has changed considerably over the last 10 years, and to make sure that a law department is not only current but *ahead* of the game, it needs to look at the future. It is time to look at the *software and hardware* of your law departments.

This chapter originally appeared in *Building the Law Department of Tomorrow*, published in October 2017.

References

1. *Building an Outstanding Legal Team: Battle-Tested Strategies from a General Counsel*, Bjarne P. Tellmann, General Counsel and Chief Legal Officer, Pearson plc. Globe Law and Business, 2017.
2. *Business @ the Speed of Thought: Succeeding in the Digital Economy*, Bill Gates. Penguin Business Library, 2000.
3. *New Directions in Legal Services*, Janvi Patel and others. ARK Group, 2017.

Chapter 7:

How to survive and succeed leading a multi-generational practice group

By Phyllis Weiss Haserot, president and founder of Practice Development Counsel

In the 1980s when the realities of having to add marketing skills to their responsibilities began to sink in, lawyers used to say, "I didn't go to school to sell". In today's ever changing legal market, and in the face of competition from new players for talent and clients, legal practice leaders may be saying, "I didn't go to school to be a human resources practitioner".

Now to maximize productivity, engagement, and a winning client experience, it's all about how you treat, train, coach, retain, and grow your talented lawyers and staff. It's about staffing matters in ways that delight clients and meet their diversity goals, anticipate their threats and opportunities, and show you truly care and make things easy for them. Whew!

And all of this must manifest with a multigenerational workforce and client team having different perspectives, wants, needs, technical expertise, behaviors, and approaches to problem-solving.

Implementing the insight and tips in this chapter will help you to:

- Build multi-generational rapport and speak with a cross-generational voice;
- Motivate lawyers to give prompt feedback and transfer knowledge;
- Help young lawyers grow into leadership responsibilities and motivate top talent to want to stay;
- Facilitate harmonious relationships among the different generations in your group and client teams; and
- Get help to perform aspects of this role you are not suited for or cannot find time for.

Challenges

Given a typical law firm compensation system, which rewards billable hours and new business production above all else, a practice group leader is bound to feel the danger of both overwhelm and tension between short-term and longer term objectives and priorities. While the pressure to attract and nurture new business and keep current clients very happy is ever present, the leader must also develop and keep the troops motivated.

Internal challenges

Many decades ago, when most associates had a shot at partnership and it was assumed that firms were a true partnership, practice leaders and seasoned partners understood that talent development was a key part of their role. There was typically more informal mentorship since associates were expected to represent the future of the firm. At the same time, associates accepted the rigid hierarchy of titles and roles and enjoyed more predictability in their careers.

Today, predictability and patience in all quarters is largely gone in terms of retaining clients as well as associates and fellow partners. With demographic shifts filling firms with lawyers from at least three or four generations with different perspectives and expectations, practice group leaders need to be re-thinking what's really important to get the job done for clients with the most appropriate talent.

According to Altman Weil's "Law Firms in Transition (2017)"[1] report 88 percent of leaders say their firm has chronically underperforming lawyers. (They are especially weak in business development skills.)

Some key structural changes leaders need to consider given desires or demands from both clients and Millennial associates are:

- Abandoning or at least loosening rigid hierarchy in assigning practice roles;
- Hastening leadership responsibilities for third year and older associates;
- Exposing second and third year associates to client contact (that is, sooner than typically implemented);
- Transparency about expectations and the path to career progress at the firm;

- Taking on "sponsorship" of senior associates and junior partners who are considered partnership high potentials in order to afford them visibility and introductions within and outside the firm;
- Continual succession planning; and
- Developing an effective feedback process.

External challenges

Practice group leaders are constantly made well aware of challenges from clients and competitors for their clients. They must take these seriously and anticipate both threats and opportunities. Considerable help can be obtained by working closely with marketing and business development professionals and *listening* to their advice.

Among the challenges practice leaders must take seriously are:

- Diversifying staffing (not just by gender) beyond the familiarity factor to meet the needs of the assignment and the client;
- Recognizing the impact of generational diversity to influence other diversity factors;
- The desires and demands of Gen X and Millennial clients differing from Baby Boomer clients; and
- Keeping clients and allied professionals aware of changes in staffing and leadership as early as possible, avoiding all surprises as much as possible.

Solutions

Recognizing that change is hard – but self-initiated change is easier to take than forced change – here are recommendations for practice leaders to swim ahead of the tsunami building from the inside and outside.

- *Loosen up!* Abandon rigid hierarchy and assess needed attributes and skills for each situation to designate who is best for each role. Not only are the younger generations impatient, but also they don't necessarily observe traditional protocol when they think they have something to contribute to the conversation. Each generation will bring a different perspective and is worth considering for effective outcomes and to keep individuals motivated.
- Get serious about a frequent, timely *feedback process*. Millenials are known for wanting and expecting regular feedback; but it's actually

Gen Xers who started the feedback push in earlier years. Practice leaders should implement both formal and informal feedback systems along with mentoring as needed and an accountability process so that it is actually done by and for all generations. That will mean in many cases that feedbackers are rewarded, at least until it becomes an established part of the group and firm culture.

- Make *career growth paths* tangible. Desired talent wants to know the firm and leader expectations and the path to achieving whatever goals they set. Instead of the historically vague or secretive criteria for progression, be transparent and as specific as possible. This may include internal lateral (lattice pattern) moves, since law firms are relatively flat organizations. Role shifts may be needed for seasoned attorneys as well as junior ones. Role shifts should not be regarded as demotions but rather opportunities to make valuable contributions, learn new things, and enhance the careers of productive lawyers.
- Related to career paths and group sustainability is the all-important need for continual *succession planning and knowledge transfer* for all critical positions. This should be one of the most important tasks for practice leaders and is too often neglected, especially at the group level. This requires a long-term vision mentality on the part of the practice group leaders and continual attention to avoiding incentives or inclinations for hoarding knowledge and preventing exposure to clients.[2]
- Give *young professionals opportunities* to test out leadership responsibilities and have a voice regarding things that affect them. Don't limit more junior colleagues by "protecting them" to stay dependent on you. Provide training and coaching; make them feel challenged and important. Increase their (soft) relationship skills. The more you support young colleagues to grow, the stronger the group will be and the lighter your production and managerial burden.
- Keep *older group members engaged* so they don't want to leave or sabotage new ideas.

Action steps to manage change

An effective practice group leader in a multi-generational workplace and market must develop rapport with people of each generation. One aspect is to realize that level in the firm doesn't directly correlate with generational attributes and behaviors. Yet while individuals differ, there are some typical patterns to anticipate by generation. Knowing and being guided by them will help to elicit cooperation and best effort from group members. Here's a cheat sheet that can start you down a productive path of working well together.

Generational rapport building blocks

Several guidelines apply for all intergenerational interactions with clients, colleagues, and new acquaintances:

- Don't make assumptions. Ask questions, and then listen carefully;
- Be respectful, and avoid arrogance;
- Flex your style to use others' communication styles and media;
- Look for things to learn from and teach to each other; and
- Find interests beyond your work, and learn from them with curiosity and interest.

Beyond these basics, there are specific good practices to follow with each generation that create the impression you can work effectively together.

For Boomer and Gen X rapport with Millennials:

- Treat them as individuals rather than as part of a "class" with a label;
- Paint the big picture for them about their role or what you are asking them to do;
- Be transparent and authentic;
- Give them feedback and recognition – frequently (most crave it);
- Keep them in the loop and conversation;
- Expect their desire for flexibility;
- Show interest in learning from them;
- Make introductions to your network of colleagues; and
- Establish reverse and mutual mentoring.

For Millennials rapport with Boomers:

- Show initiative;
- Convey confidence without arrogance;
- Establish relationships in person, if possible;
- Ask how you can best help them, clients, and colleagues;
- Answer their questions fully;
- Recognize their achievements (they are proud of them);
- Show interest in learning from them – partake in reverse and mutual mentoring; and
- Share your interests and learn about theirs openly.

For any generation with Gen Xers:

- Respect their time. It's a form of currency (like money) to them;
- Have specific goals. Lay out plans. Have data to back up assertions;
- Don't expect automatic loyalty. You will have to earn it. Expect skepticism;
- Don't micro-manage them. Give them options;
- Learn to ask for and give feedback; and
- Appreciate that they place high priority on family and friends.

For other generations with Traditionalists (the generation older than Boomers):

- Take time to educate them. Expect that once persuaded, they will be loyal;
- Minimize the use of technology in communication, and make it personal; and
- Emphasize courtesy and be personable.

How to speak with a cross-generational voice

All leaders will benefit from using the above tips on building cross-generational rapport.

If you are a new practice group leader, you have the opportunity to make changes with a fresh start. Use your powers of reflection, and do your homework.

- Think back to what you liked about how a practice group to which you belonged functioned, and what you didn't like, whether it was the same group as your current one or another. What worked? What practices, policies, and behaviors motivated group members, made the group productive, and delighted clients?
- Have one-on-one talks with each group member to get their views on the above questions. Understand what is important to each group member. Millennials and younger Gen Xers will especially appreciate being given a voice and your openness to change. Members of older generations will appreciate your attention to them as playing an ongoing important role in the group or a new role as a mentor, coach, or elder statesperson for important clients, for example.
- Establish relationships with the most important clients your group serves, and use the tips to develop rapport with people of each generation. Encourage relationship nurturing between group members of each generation and their client peers.
- Don't over-focus on any one generation (e.g., Millennials) and neglect the others. That will be noticed and set an example.
- Institute a series of facilitated dialogues within the practice group and, if appropriate with others on relevant client teams. For these dialogues, participate as just one of the group members, and bring in a neutral facilitator.[3]

If you are a seasoned practice group leader, the action steps above apply for the ongoing leader as well. However, there are special wrinkles (no pun intended) when you aren't starting with a clean slate. Since group members will have formed expectations about how the group will operate, there may be resistance to change and ingrained relationships to contend with.

- Assess other groups in the firm that may have a role model that could work for your group as far as increased productivity and satisfaction for members. Use that model's success to develop buy-in, and give resisters significant roles in the new model.

- Carefully consider the appropriateness of generational match-ups with clients. Studies have found firm leaders are often significantly older than most of their clients.
- Sponsor younger attorneys in the group for visibility and leadership. They will become allies.
- Even if the firm doesn't have a formal succession planning and knowledge transfer process, establish one for the group. Don't view this as a threat to your position. If you institute it, you are likely to retain a role in the process and future vision.

Help!

As described, this is too big a job for one person. Not every practice group leader is temperamentally or substantively suited to take on, for example, the human resources aspect of the role. Admit there are some aspects of the practice group leader job you are not suited to do, don't want to do, or can't make time for. Hand those parts over to someone who can better fulfil those parts of the role and "let go".

How do you find help to share the burden of this big job?

- Be honest with yourself about what you do best and like doing;
- Define aspects you and the group would benefit from your delegating;
- Identify which aspects can be given to younger group members for potential leadership training and to elicit new ideas;
- Identify what help can productively come from non-lawyer staff in the firm such as marketing, business development, finance, human resources, professional development trainers, IT staff; and
- Keep in mind the critical need to communicate early and often and clearly, with those you delegate to as well as directly to your team. You are still responsible for the overall performance and behavior of the group.

Lastly, and very importantly, find ways to relieve the stress of the big job, and enjoy the journey!

This chapter originally appeared in *Effective Practice Group Leadership*, published in September 2017.

References

1. Altman Weil, "Law Firms in Transition 2017", April 2017. See: http://www.altmanweil.com/LFiT2017/
2. Practice Development Counsel's free assessment tool, "Barriers to Knowledge Transfer" is available from pwhaserot@pdcounsel.com.
3. A case study on facilitated work team dialogues is available from pwhaserot@pdcounsel.com.

Part three: Finance

Chapter 8: Promoting firm goals through effective associate compensation approaches

By Arthur G Greene, principal, Boyer Greene, LLC

The topic of associate compensation involves more than setting the salary. The associate's value to the firm will depend on other factors than picking a number. Let's remember that, in most cases, the reason for employing associates includes the contribution they will bring to advancing the firm's strategic plan and achieving the firm's goals. For the associate, the focus will include how they can advance their career objectives. Only by addressing both factors can the firm and the associate achieve their respective goals.

Unlike larger firms with integrated approaches, many small and mid-sized firms struggle with the uncertainty as to whether their approaches are effective in advancing the goals of the firm. Too often, smaller firms simply want to identify the salary arrangement that will either attract a candidate to the firm or cause a current associate to stay with the firm.

Some firms utilize the traditional approach of paying a base salary and a discretionary bonus. Other firms may apply more direct, incentive-based methods that are often designed by firm management to meet some perceived need to motivate associates. And then, there is the worst case – some firms create chaos by designing a different arrangement for each associate.

An integrated approach to associate compensation

Associate compensation is not a stand-alone consideration. Most associates regard their career development as more important than the amount of their compensation. This can come as a surprise to many partners. What managing partners need to know is that surveys have shown that the majority of associate turnover is caused by a lack of training and/or commitment to their career development. This has been determined to be true, even in many cases where associates give their reason for leaving a firm as moving on to make more money.

From the law firm's standpoint, the most meaningful contribution an associate can make requires them to have an understanding of the firm's goals and its strategic plan. Associates will be more content and better invested if they understand their role and the contributions they can make to help the firm reach its goals. To limit the information provided to them serves to isolate associates and prevents them from making a greater contribution.

Meaningful communication is often missing. This may include sharing (i) the partners' expectations of the associate, (ii) how the firm can assist the associate in developing their careers, (iii) how the associate will be evaluated on an annual basis and given constructive suggestions, and (iv) the associate's role in advancing the firm's goals and strategic plan. Withholding information from the associates, whether intentional or an oversight, is both common and results in a negative impact in a firm's relationship with its associates.

The integration of these factors into an associate compensation approach will assure an effective associate program with the proper incentives. Getting the salary amount right is important, but that is only one step in the process. An integrated approach will increase associate satisfaction, thereby reducing turnover, and will better prepare associates for partnership opportunities.

Methods of associate compensation

The first thought most lawyers have when considering associate compensation is what other firms in the region pay. While compensation may be market-driven, particularly in large firms, other factors that apply in small and mid-sized firms may include lifestyle and culture, the nature of the work, or partnership opportunities.

Salary plus discretionary bonus

The most traditional method of compensating an associate is a salary plus a discretionary bonus. In firms utilizing this approach, it is common to have 80–95 percent of the compensation paid during the year as salary. A discretionary bonus is paid at year-end based on a subjective analysis of the associate's performance during the year, considering such factors as the quality of their work, meeting productivity requirements, professional development, and the associate's contribution to the advancement of the firm's goals.

This method reserves to the partners the most control over the associate and his/her work. Communication is important, which means the associate needs to know what expectations are considered in setting salary and/or the bonus.

Salary plus incentive bonus

Some firms have data-based formulas for paying a bonus to associates. These arrangements may result in leaving anywhere from 10-50 percent of the overall compensation in the bonus category. The financial rewards can be for (i) meeting or exceeding billable hour requirements, (ii) exceeding revenue expectations, or (iii) achieving a designated level of originations.

Comments on various approaches

There are an unlimited number of variations of the basic models. All firms are different. The following comments are provided to assist in evaluating what approach will work best for your firm.

Large firm approaches

The larger the firm, the more likely it will have a compensation system not unlike any big business. Salaries are subjectively set based on meeting performance standards, after an evaluation process involving either an associate committee, a practice group chair, or both.

- *Large firm advantage.* The largest and most successful firms can afford to attract the best candidates. They operate at a different level and tend to be more structured and organized than smaller firms.
- *A signing bonus.* In order to attract the best candidates and get an edge on the competition, some large firms pay a signing bonus to the associate. The amount may vary and it could be $5K on signing and an additional $5K on the first day of work.
- *Lock-step compensation.* Some firms have lock-step systems with salary ranges within each step. The associate may move from step-to-step based upon seniority or, in the alternative, based on performance. The range gives decision-makers the ability to reward or penalize an associate within that level based on performance. The lock-step avoids the potential for difficulty of making it up from year to year, associate to associate.
- *Discretionary bonuses.* Discretionary bonuses are most common because it allows the firm to set expectations based on a broad range of factors. Discretionary bonuses also provide the firm with the most flexibility and control over the associates.

- *Incentive bonuses.* Some large firms provide set bonus amounts for exceeding billable hour requirements, revenue production expectations, or the amount of originations. While these can work well in some instances, the downside may be the possibility that the associate feels decisions about their performance level have been delegated to them.
- *Partnership policy.* All large firms have set policies as to the opportunity for partnership. The policy will include the number of years and the criteria that need to be met to qualify for partnership status. Every associate knows on the first day what the opportunity is and how they might achieve partnership status. If the firm is one that provides for lifetime non-partner status, that needs to be spelled out as well.

Small firm approaches

One disadvantage of small firm approaches to associate compensation is they tend to make it up as they go along. Unfortunately, some of the approaches that are taken may be based more on the firm's limited financial resources than on what approach would best serve the firm and its goals for the future. Unusual arrangements can lead to associate turnover.

- *Salary and discretionary bonus.* This standard approach is both common and most successful in small and mid-sized firms. The key to success is communication. The associate needs to know what the partners' performance expectations are and how their performance will advance their career development and the goals of the firm. Constructive annual performance reviews are critical and should address progress for meeting partnership criteria by year three.
- *Incentivized methods.* Partners in small and mid-sized firms should carefully consider why they are utilizing formula-based systems for some or all of the associate's compensation. Is it because they cannot run the risk of committing to a salary? Or is it because they are trying to get the associate to perform in a certain way? Why is a direct incentive based on a formula better than an incentive imposed by a discretionary bonus? Is it because the firm cannot effectively manage the associates' performances through setting expectations, tracking results, and subjectively incentivizing with salary adjustment and discretionary bonuses?

- In some small firms, formula-based approaches have caused unintended consequences. There are questions to ask before employing these formulas. Do you really want associates focused more on the number of hours recorded than on the quality of their work? Do you want associates working on marginal matters they originated at the expense of more lucrative work that the firm needs to advance? Importantly, do you want the associate thinking that he or she gets to decide how hard they work based on the compensation level that they may find satisfying? While these incentives may be appropriate under some circumstances, the instances are rare. Regardless of their good attentions, many firms find direct incentives for associates problematic. Too often, firms resort to these approaches when they cannot pay an adequate base salary.
- *Standardization.* The most successful associate compensation systems in small and mid-sized firms involve a carefully crafted standardized approach, including good communication and time invested in mentoring, evaluating, and giving significant attention to associate career development.

Integrating all aspects of the associate program

As the firm considers the method of compensation, it should not overlook integrating the other aspects of an effective associate program. The better the structure of the overall associate program, the fewer dollars alone it may take to attract the best candidates available.

Training and mentoring

Be prepared to describe to the associate the firm's training and mentoring program. This will have more to do with retaining associates than having to pay a little extra. Do not underestimate the importance of working with associates to assist them in becoming better lawyers and advancing their career to achieve their potential. And, of course, the firm needs to deliver, which is sometimes harder to accomplish than just talking about training and mentoring.

Transparency

The most successful law firms are good at planning. Successful firms hold annual retreats for partners to focus on strategic planning. The process involves identifying core values, creating a mission statement, and developing a vision for the future. Once the firm knows where it wants to be in five or ten years, a strategic plan will provide the roadmap for achieving the vision. Regardless of whether the partners develop a sophisticated strategic plan, or have informally identified what they hope to accomplish, having a plan is important.

The plan needs to consist of more than loose ideas or a document kept in a desk drawer. The plan needs to be realistic, kept alive, and shared with everyone in the firm. Associates should be aware of the firm's strategic plan and understand that they have a role in helping the firm achieve its goals.

Associate evaluations

Associates need to understand (i) what the partners expect of them, (ii) how they can contribute to the success of the firm, and (iii) how they are progressing as lawyers. While communications through day-to-day comments and suggestions are critical, annual associate evaluations are the necessary method for guiding associates through their growth as lawyers and valuable members of the firm.

Lawyer annual plans

The lawyer annual plan is considered an essential tool for managing lawyers. The lawyer annual plan is not limited to associates. It is critical in coordinating the efforts of all lawyers, including partners.

Lawyer annual plans bring together associate career development and law firm strategic plans. Each associate (and partner) is required to develop an annual plan, with significant input from management before it is finalized. The annual plans become important in assisting the managing partner's efforts to have all firm needs covered in a coordinated manner. If every lawyer successfully executes their annual plan, the goals of the firm will be met.

The following process should be followed:

- Each lawyer should complete a first draft of an annual plan. (See Figure 1 overleaf for a sample.)
- The managing partner (or some other designated manager) will meet with the lawyer to discuss the plan and then make any modifications agreed upon during the discussion.
- The completed annual plans should be maintained by the individual lawyer and the managing partner.
- The lawyer should create an action list to assist in monitoring progress.

- At least quarterly, the individual lawyer and managing partner should meet to assess the progress being made and note further actions necessary to achieve the goals of the plan.

Lawyer annual plan

Lawyer ________________________________ Year ____________

Concentration of your practice with approved changes.

Expectations with regard to service of clients.

Agreed plan to:

- Enhance your skills
- Expand your practice
- Improve your productivity
- Assist others in improving their practices
- Assume responsibilities within the firm
- Advance the goals of the firm
- Participate in civic and professional matters

Productivity expectations:

Billable hours_________ Originations $_________

Client files managed $_________ Realization _________%

Accepted by lawyer: ____

Approved by managing partner: ______________________________

Dated: January ______, 20____

Figure 1: Example of a lawyer annual plan.

The annual plans can be monitored on a monthly or quarterly basis, so shortfalls can be identified and corrected before it is too late in the year. A review at year-end to evaluate whether the expectations set out in the plan have been met can be a significant aspect in determining bonuses and/or in setting salaries for the following year.

Each firm should consider the sample above as a starting point to developing a form that will work best for the firm. Sections may include some or all of the following, if applicable:

- Personal production goals:
  - Billable hours;
  - Estimate the revenue generation from the billed hours; and
  - Description of non-billable contributions.
- Personal practice goals:
  - Continuing legal education (CLE) to enhance practice skills; and
  - Strategies to improve practice skills and client service skills.
- Production enhancement goals:
- Efforts to improve individual production including:
  - Increasing hourly rate(s);
  - Increasing efficiencies;
  - Leveraging/delegation; and
  - Increasing client base.
- Firm management efforts:
  - Contributions to the development and training of younger lawyers in the firm;
  - Contributions regarding the overall firm management efforts; and
  - Efforts to be made to enhance leadership and management skills and abilities.
- Individual lawyer and firm client development efforts:
  - Cross-selling efforts to enhance the overall firm new work generation effort;
  - Client development, marketing goals, objectives, and strategies;
  - New clients, new referral sources, and new markets that will be a focus; and
  - Contributions to the overall firm marketing effort.

Once the annual plans have been finalized, they should be consistently tracked by the managing partner, with the assistance of the firm administrator (or others delegated by management to have a role in this process).

Partner track or contract associates

Every firm should have partner track associates. First generation firms wait until too late to realize that partner track associates may be critical to the senior lawyers' exit plans and to the continuity of the firm. Ignoring succession issues until the founders are well into their sixties is doomed to failure. For a firm to be considered healthy, there should be a succession plan, which means a second generation of partners ready to transition into the lead roles in the firm.

A succession plan means associates are made aware of the opportunity and understand the criteria they need to meet to be considered for partnership. Firms that are silent on the issue are often subjected to high levels of associate turnover.

In most firms, every associate has an opportunity to become a partner if he/she meets the firm's criteria for partner status. As noted, surveys have shown that many associates are more concerned about career development than the amount of their weekly paycheck. It is important to let associates know from the start what the opportunity is and what it takes to achieve it.

At the same time, there are young lawyers who are not motivated by a partnership opportunity. In fact, they may want to practice law at their pace, without the stress and obligations of having an ownership interest in the firm. Every firm needs potential successors, but some firms do provide for contract positions, in certain circumstances, for a limited number of lawyers. The risk is the possibility of ending up with too many contract lawyers and too few successors. If that happens, surviving into the next generation becomes unlikely.

Recommendations

In developing an approach to associate compensation, firm management needs to address the following issues:

- Do we have a job description for the role we are trying to fill?
- Where will the work for the associate come from?
- What are the productivity expectations, and how will the associate contribute to the firm's goals and strategic plan?
- How much transparency of office workings are we prepared to share with the associates?
- Do we have an adequate training and mentoring program that we have confidence in as we describe it to the associate?

- Is our associate annual review process adequate?
- Can we institute a lawyer annual plan process in helping the associate understand our expectations and guide his or her career?
- Is there any reason a traditional salary plus discretionary bonus would not be the best approach? If not, why not, and would there be any unintended consequences in any formula-based method we consider?

Final thoughts

Remember, setting associate compensation involves more than choosing a salary. The process needs to include methods for achieving firm goals, incentivizing proper behaviors, and retaining the lawyer long-term. Effective communication makes the difference between success and failure. The importance of an integrated approach to associate compensation cannot be overstated.

There are several approaches to choose from in setting associate compensation, and no one model fits every firm. The method needs to be tailored to the individual firm, but in every case, promoting the success of the firm in achieving its goals should be paramount.

This chapter originally appeared in *Compensation Innovation: An in-depth exploration into the future of law firm compensation*, published in March 2018.

Chapter 9:
A data scientist's perspective on law firm profitability

By Zev J Eigen, founder and chief science officer of Syndio Solutions

Introduction

My name is Zev Eigen, and I'm a former (recovering) law professor and current data scientist. I've worked at and with large and small law firms for more than two decades. I've served as in-house counsel for a large entertainment industry studio. I've also been in the trenches with fellow data science and technophilic evangelists trying to preach to law firm leaders that there is money to be made – vast sums of it, in fact – if they would just turn their firms into things that they are not; if they would only listen to reason and completely revamp their compensation structures to properly incentivize innovation; and of course, if they hire data scientists (not more lawyers or firm management specialists), give them a budget and a seat at the table in order to develop and implement firm strategy. See – that's not hard, right?

And so it goes, with firm leadership almost universally and exclusively making small incremental changes within the confines of existing inefficient organizational infrastructures. Big functional changes that question the very existential identity of a "law firm" are few and far between. I call these small changes "faster horses" innovation, as a reference to the famed quote attributed to Henry Ford: "If I had asked people what they wanted, they would have said faster horses." If you ask lawyers and law firm leaders what they need to innovate, they will tell you faster lawyers, better e-discovery, or a better billing system. It's rare that they would suggest artificial intelligence systems to automate the delivery of legal services, or a SaaS (that's "software as a service") model of delivery of automatable output that could render some of the work lawyers are doing and billing for obsolete. The idea of decreasing billable hours is lauded in public in front of clients, and derided in private as the sounding of a death knell for the practice of law.

In the midst of the quasi-technology revolution occurring now – where the rate of innovation lauded at #LegalTech conferences is significantly greater than the actual rate of innovation – some firms are starting to embrace the idea of using data to improve processes. If you're not a lawyer or you haven't worked at a large law firm, your reaction to that statement is undoubtedly: "Of course everyone uses data to improve processes." However, the idea of law firms tracking key performance metrics, analyzing those data and then using the output of that analysis to render strategic decisions at a firm is *huge*. In the anachronistic space of law firm leadership and management, making big decisions based on things outside of one's experience, intuition, subject matter expertise is really foreign.

I will offer two readily available forms of innovation that firms are adopting now. First, I'll describe a "faster horses" form of innovation – a means of improving how the firm functions to deliver existing offerings (billable hours). I'll then describe a "new car" form of innovation that firms are offering to their clients – in the form of a SaaS solution.

The fastest of fast horses: improving collaboration with relational data

One way in which firms are beginning to figure this out is by leveraging the power of "relational data". Across the way, in the HR tech space, we are experiencing a data scientific revolution. That means that big HR problems are being addressed by new sources of higher quality data, and those data are being cultivated into actionable business intelligence for companies wise enough to incorporate next generation HR Tech into their toolkits. One of the biggest ways in which this revolution is being staged is by the gathering and evaluation of *relational* data. Relational data are measures of how people interact to get work done. By contrast, *attribute* data are measures that describe what people are. Attribute data include measures like educational attainment, tenure on the job, skill sets, etc. Relational data include measures like whether people are connected to each other, how much they rely on each other for information or support, how much they inspire each other, or how well they collaborate with each other. When work consisted of linear hierarchies and reporting, and people spent their whole careers at one job, often in one or two geographic locations in close proximity to the rest of the company, attribute data were more useful. Work doesn't look like that anymore. Not by a long shot. Work is decentralized, global, and there is less reliance on standard hierarchical structures. People work on devices from anywhere and at any time of day. This is especially true for the practice of law. Pressures from clients are ensuring that the trend of decentralization continues. A big part of the data scientific revolution is the realization that relational data are much better suited than attribute data at solving the biggest and most costly HR problems.

	Attribute Data	**Relational Data**
Examples:	Job tenure, educational attainment	Connections among people, how much A collaborates with B
Description:	Identifying statistical comparisons (e.g.: is there a relationship between educational attainment and turn-over?)	Measuring how work gets done, where collaboration is successful or not, and tying that to bottom-line measures of profitability
Unit of Analysis:	Individual	Individual & Groups
Origins:	HRIS, application process, employee surveys	Employee surveys, meta-data derived from email, calendar and IM
USE CASE EFFICACY RATING:		
Selection	B-	N/A
Performance Management	B	A
Collaboration	B	A+
Predicting turnover	B+	A-
Improving Inclusion as part of a Diversity & Inclusion Initiative	B	A+
Change management	B-	A+
Identifying the most influential people at an organization	F	A+

Figure 1: Comparison of attribute and relational data.

Another important component of the HR tech revolution we are currently experiencing is the renewed focus and attention being paid to collaboration. There is so much evidence of the direct link between the right kinds of collaboration and objective measures and bottom line profit across a diverse array of organizational contexts. For instance, Professors Brian Uzzi and Jarrett Spiro demonstrated that finding the right kind and amount of collaboration increased the likelihood that a

Broadway musical would be profitable.[1] They looked at 45 years' worth of musicals. Collaboration in the hospitality industry produces happier guests. There is a lot of attention paid recently to the ways in which collaboration at law firms produces greater profit. For instance, Heidi Gardner, a professor at Harvard Law School and former consultant, has written extensively about how law firms should be gathering and analyzing relational data in order to drive profitability. She evaluated billing records from several large firms over time to show the consistent connection between collaboration and success.

Even at hospitals, the doctor-nurse teams that collaborate better are more likely to generate better patient outcomes. In that case, better collaboration could literally mean the difference between life and death. Across all of these diverse organizational settings (creative arts, hospitality, legal services and medical services), humans have to work with other humans to produce some output. It should not be surprising, then, that understanding the interconnectedness among people via relational data analytics is the A+ method for driving bottom line profitability in so many diverse organizational settings.

Even when law firms spend millions of dollars renovating physical spaces to induce "better collaboration," very little is often done to deliberately measure which groups are collaborating better than others. How do you know that the spaces are cultivated collaboration? How do you know that you've assigned work on teams with optimal collaborative potential? How do you know which teams of lawyers require coaching to improve collaboration? Without measuring collaboration and using the data to create the right constellation of groups, employers are missing out on the tremendous cost savings and profit generation potential. There is ample empirical social scientific evidence that would make the value proposition of investing in tools to accurately measure collaboration and to enable the deliberate optimization of teams a "no-brainer".

There are a variety of effective and most efficient methods for gathering, analyzing and reporting relational data at organizations, including a tool developed by the team at Syndio. Survey instruments are available that enable employees to report critical information about how work gets done. Where appropriate or necessary, these platforms take in email and calendar meta-data as a proxy for quantity of digital communication. "Under the hood," a barrage of sophisticated measures are calculated to gauge how well individuals are collaborating and where they are failing to sufficiently collaborate. Those measures are then visualized on easy to understand dashboards. The dashboards are designed to ensure that the data are transformed into actionable business intelligence. For instance,

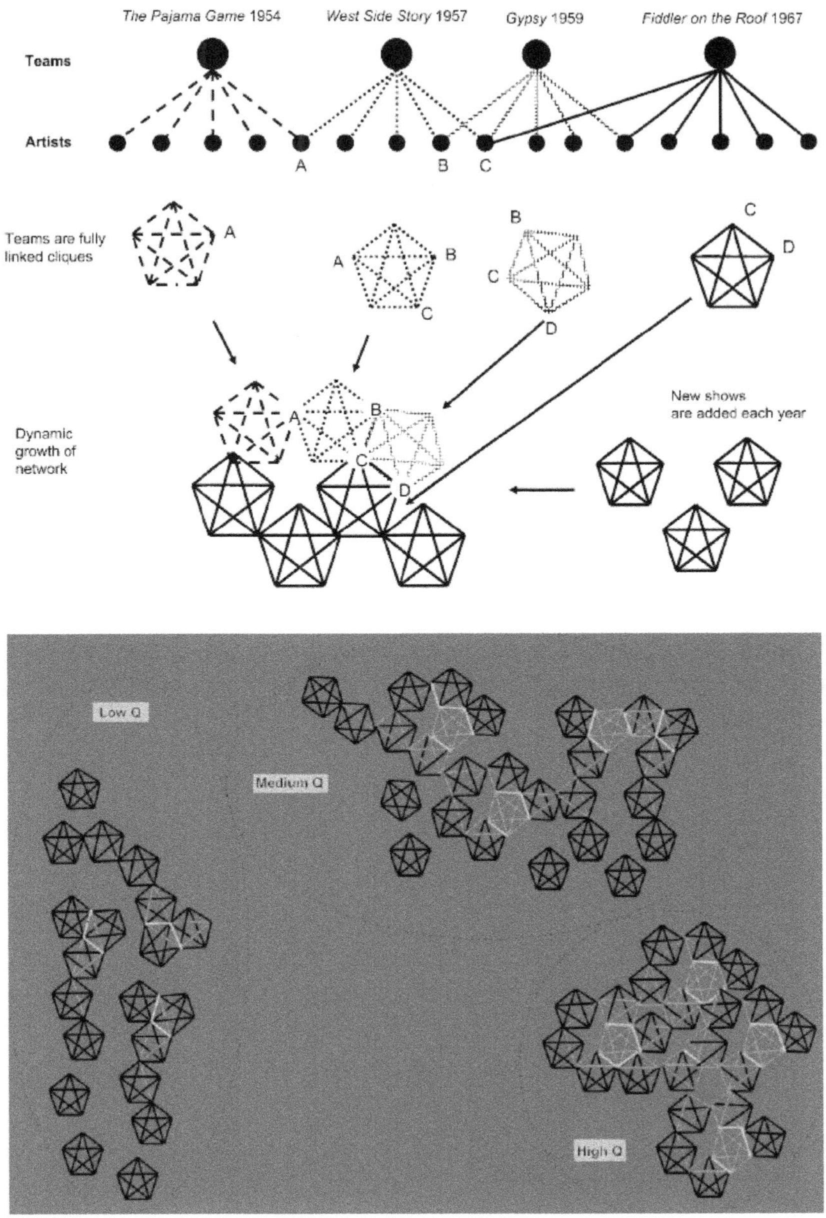

Figure 2: Uzzi and Sprio show that it takes the right quantity and quality of collaboration to produce profitable Broadway musicals.

the dashboard output empowers HR leaders to answer the following critical questions:

1. Which groups are the most cohesive? Which groups are the least cohesive?
2. What is the relationship between collaboration and measurable bottom line profit?
3. Which individuals are suffering from "collaborative overload" (a form of suboptimal over-utilization often associated with highly influential employees feeling burnt out)?

Once the survey instrument is deployed, and the data received analyzed, the dashboard empowers business leaders to address these questions head-on and then implement meaningful change that has an empirically demonstrable impact on bottom-line profitability. Some users employ these data to identify high collaboration and low collaboration groups, forming strategies on how to make the lower performing groups collaborate more. That could mean simply enabling some lesser collaboration individuals to work with the high-collaboration individuals as a way of training them to improve. There are many great ways to use this kind of dashboard information to improve collaboration and reduce collaborative load.

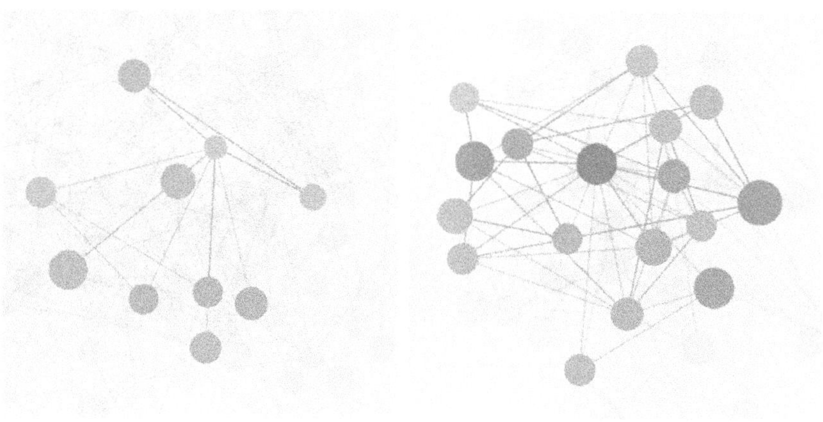

Figure 3: Examples of a low collaboration team and a high collaboration team; the latter was significantly more profitable before intervention and coaching.

It is truly the case that, as part of the data science revolution in HR, many better tools are now readily available to employers wise enough to take advantage of them. Relational data scientific platforms, like Syndio's, offer precisely this solution. As a data scientist and someone who has worked very hard for more than two decades to find the right data sources to solve the biggest HR problems, I love watching how quickly and easily these tools enable the capture and maximization of value through measuring collaboration across diverse organizational settings.

The new car: closing the gender pay gap with SaaS

Law firms are just starting to transform the way they offer the services they've traditionally sold to clients. Four factors are pushing and pulling firms towards software as a service ("SaaS") and related alternative technological offerings that are fundamentally better than traditional attorney work. Firstly, the pipeline of talent is drying up as the best of the best opt for business school, entrepreneurship, engineering or other STEM fields instead of law school. This is because the value proposition for attending law school has shifted. It is unlikely the optimum alternative for smart students looking for a grad school opportunity. As the talent pool shrinks, the need for alternatives to labor grows. Secondly, clients are demanding different forms of service offerings, focused on solving business problems. Greater resources are being put into in-house legal teams, reducing the need for costly external counsel for some types of legal work. Clients are loath to pay for work that they know can be automated. Thirdly, increased competition from alternative service providers has firms more wisely mindful of encroachment on their turf. Fourthly, the cohort of firm leaders currently in place are being replaced by the newer cohort of leaders. For the previous group, the model they know and love has always worked, and they are loath to change something proactively. It is like a leader of a yellow taxi cab company being confronted by rising popularity and market share loss due to ride sharing upstarts. They know their model works because of the past, and they don't want to change a thing. Newer leaders see the practice of law as a business first, not a learned profession first. That means closer adherence to profit and loss models, reliance on data for decision making, and a willingness to change incentive structures and offer more innovative optimal things that clients demand.

While there are several ways for firms to offer the "new car" to clients, one that makes a lot of sense is gender pay equity review work. Clients may want legal advice on how to comply with the burgeoning array of federal, state and international laws requiring companies to pay men and women the same for substantially similar work. There are legal issues like, "Which employees should be grouped together for the sake of rendering comparisons?", "What is the proper measure of compensation?" and "What are legally defensible explanatory measures like tenure or educational attainment that may be applied to account for problematic gaps identified?" Aside from those legal questions, the vast majority of the work required is math, data analytics, and diagnostic descriptive statistics and visualizations. The laws do not require a showing of intent. Most of the review process may be handled algorithmically. A software as a service solution is perfect.

Firms may surely opt to build their own version of a SaaS solution; however, this is almost invariably a suboptimal option for three reasons. Firstly, software development is not a one-and-done thing, especially for something like this. There are significant ongoing costs associated with this undertaking. Firms routinely underestimate these costs because they have created other small apps on their websites. They lack the required experience to know how to accurately forecast costs. Conversely, software developers are not experts at forecasting legal costs. Secondly, there are significant expertise required to build a good pay equity analysis tool. Firms don't know what they don't know about building a tool for this purpose. Thirdly, firms are not properly set up to staff around the deployment of SaaS. This requires dedicated customer success, technical support, sales support, deployment experts, and related personnel. In short, the option to build something may seem tempting but, in the long run, it will involve greater than expected expenditure to result in a less than imagined product that requires more care and upkeep than expected.

There is a readily available solution: partner with a vendor which is singularly focused on developing the best available SaaS solution, and pair it with legal services offered to your clients. It is scalable, low-cost, and highly efficient. It offers technology that is in high demand by clients and opportunities to showcase the firm's legitimate commitment to innovation. This is a clear path to optimizing profitability. The firm reduces its cost to bring something of high value to the available pool of clients. It may leverage the technology that's already been developed and is continuously improved upon by world-class data scientists, statisticians and programmers. As such, this is an ideal example of an opportunity to build and deploy innovative technology in a way that is a true win-win. The firm and the client are significantly better off.

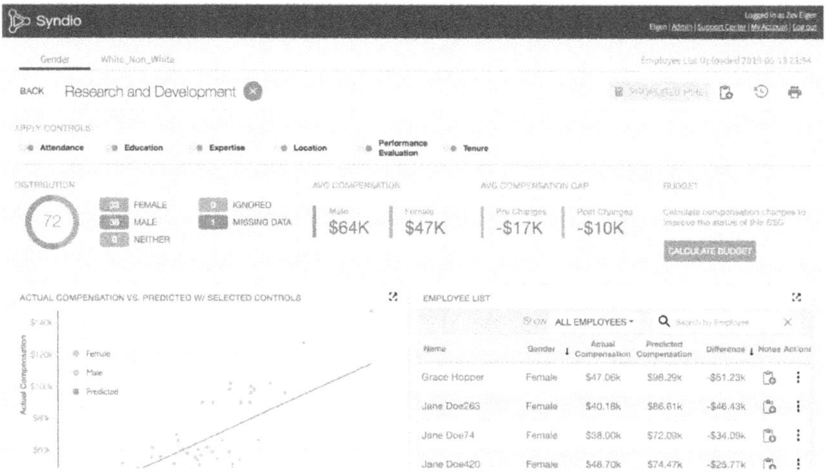

Figure 4: Screenshot from Syndio's Pay Equity Solution.

Conclusion

Firms struggle to innovate – a fact which is at the core of the profitability dilemma. Law firms want to get ahead, but they are afraid to be at the front of the pack. They are ill-equipped to properly vet opportunities and often are not properly incentivized. They fall victim of the classic economic problem known as "agency costs," in which what is in the best interest of the agents (lawyers) is not aligned with what is in the best interests of the principal (the firm). For making the firm's functioning more efficient and more profitable (based on empirical evidence) technology that measures collaboration has proven to be highly effective.

There is even a way forward in the faster cars category. Pay equity partnerships with vendors can be accomplished in baby-steps to demonstrate value. For instance, it is easy for a lawyer at a firm to identify several clients and experiment. License with a pay equity SaaS solution and measure the return on investment. Our experience indicates that clients are very pleased and lawyers make significantly more profit than if they had not offered this work or attempted to do it by hand with experts or analysts, or if they tried to handle the work any other way. As the old saying goes, "let the devil take the hindmost." Law firms that swiftly advance to the front of the herd instead of waiting for their competitors to overtake them will reap the spoils of their efforts sooner and more robustly.

This chapter originally appeared in *Emerging Approaches to Law Firm Profitability*, published in May 2018.

Reference

1. www.kellogg.northwestern.edu/faculty/uzzi/ftp/uzzi's_research_papers/0900904.pdf

Part four: Strategy

Chapter 10: Adopting a strategic planning approach and leadership for innovation

By Christie Guimond, senior manager, legal project management, White & Case

Innovation is the latest trend in the legal industry and there are countless debates as to what the term means and whether there is a real imperative to innovate – the so-called "burning platform". Regardless of how you define innovation, it is clear that the industry is facing challenges related to technology disruption, changing buyer behaviors, and increasingly competitive legal markets. The degree to which these challenges are driving legal organizations to innovate varies but many of these challenges are new for the industry, and overcoming them can require new and creative solutions. This need for creativity has caused many legal businesses to consider their approach to innovation, including who should lead it and where it should sit within the organization.

It is an emerging trend in the legal industry to create specific leadership roles (e.g. chief innovation officers and innovation managers), and/or dedicated teams, to lead their innovation efforts. However, others have sought to distribute responsibility for innovation more widely amongst their employees, harnessing ideas through committees or champions. The chapter will identify the leadership models that are currently being adopted in the legal industry and explore some of the potential pros and cons of each of these models.

While there are some tangible examples of successful innovation from legal organizations who have adopted specific innovation leadership models, the long-term sustainability of these approaches has yet to be tested. However, it is instructive to learn from examples in other industries that have much longer histories of structuring for innovation. This chapter will explore Eastman Kodak's model for innovation leadership, and will explore why this model led to their ultimate organizational failure.

It will then look at how your innovation leadership can avoid a similar fate by using a two-part strategic planning approach for innovation that considers: (1) your current position as an organization; and (2) where you want and need to go in the future.

Innovate or die – the Eastman Kodak story

There are countless stories about companies who failed to innovate, and who ultimately disappeared from the industries they once dominated, but the favorite trope amongst those who make innovation a profession is the former film and camera titan, Eastman Kodak Company. As the oft-told narrative goes, a Kodak employee who was employed in its research lab, Steven Sasson, invented a revolutionary new piece of technology – the predecessor of the digital camera. This was 1975, long before digital camera technology would gain the ubiquity it now has, and, as the story goes, Kodak failed to recognize the breakthrough nature of this technology and the digital camera never saw the light of day as one of its products. Because of this fateful decision by Leadership, Kodak slowly began to lose its grip on its market leading position as more and more customers turned away from printed photos towards digital, and today has largely faded from view in the industry it once dominated.[1]

This is a cautionary tale to any who turn a blind eye to disruption, though Kodak's Luddite reputation is not entirely an earned one. In reality, Kodak had long been an innovative company with a history of pivoting, moving from its original photo-plate technology to film and from black and white photos to color. Kodak also institutionalized innovation through dedicated R&D labs, which received significant funding to create new products and services. Contrary to popular belief, for a long period of time Kodak absolutely kept its finger on the pulse of disruption in its market, had a formal innovation structure in place, and made numerous strides to combat the threats it faced from new technologies and new entrants. From the outside, it looked like it was dealing competently with the disruption in its industry and maintained its gigantic market share long into the 2000s. Yet, despite all these efforts to innovate, it still eventually "died".

What really went wrong?

Despite Kodak's strong innovation model, its leadership failed to harness its most disruptive and valuable creation – the digital camera. The structure that the company adopted for innovation was partly to blame because it created an R&D function that fostered innovation away from the day-to-day business, but then channeled those innovations back through its traditional management decision-making processes.

The business was concerned with the day-to-day management of its short-term success,[2] and required strong business cases for any new investments. However, the digital camera, like most nascent ideas, could not prove that it would deliver return on investment in a timeframe that the business could accept. Management could not accept the risk, and chose not to develop the idea as one of its products – though it made billions from the patent in the short-term. Management also took the ultimately fatal strategic decision of trying to retrofit the underlying technology into its existing print business model. Eventually, as time would show, the real business case for digital was not just improving print quality; digital was the new business model. Unfortunately for Kodak, by the time the innovation's real value had become clear, many years later, it was too late to harness it.

Fundamentally, Kodak did not fail because it lacked a leadership model for innovation. It failed because it allowed itself to be driven by a model for innovation that did not allow it to take good strategic decisions about how to harness innovation. It is not possible to definitively say, of course, but it is plausible that the results could have been different, had the company adopted a different leadership model that was a better fit for its organizational culture and decision-making – and coupled that with a strategy for innovation that allowed it to understand and identify what it was trying achieve through innovation.

As the legal industry continues to face disruption and innovation becomes an imperative, the Kodak story is an instructive one for business leaders in legal organizations. The following section will explore how you can choose your own leadership model and develop a strategy that enables you to balance your short-term business needs with the longer term impact that disruptive innovation will have on the legal industry.

Choosing a leadership model for innovation in the legal industry

Innovation is risky and uncomfortable and, like any substantial change management effort, requires strong leadership. Top-down leadership is crucial to drive innovation, though there is no one-size-fits-all approach to innovation leadership. For some legal businesses, the appointment of a dedicated and experienced innovation expert, who lives, breathes and leads innovation (e.g a chief innovation officer, chief strategy officer, innovation/strategy manager or similar role), has helped them accelerate their innovation efforts. This approach has many benefits because it can raise the profile of innovation, provide a central point for ideas and implementation, and provide strong strategic leadership. However, it can also lead to feelings of resistance in law firms in particular given that it is a "cost center" and the returns on investment are uncertain and often difficult to quantify. Having a dedicated role or function can also lead to complacency given that innovation is someone else's "job".

Many others find that it suits their organizational culture to encourage everyone within the organization to take responsibility for innovation, to build an "innovation culture" that allows everyone to make changes at every level. This distributed and empowering approach can lead to strong feelings of engagement from many in your organization, but can also lead to a sense of detachment from those who are resistant to change and/or not naturally inclined towards innovation.

Others have found it more appropriate to allocate responsibility to existing leadership groups, to form new committees or to identify champions across the business to encourage innovation. This model can be very effective in large, global organizations because it provides critical mass to lead innovation to an extent that a single chief innovation manager could not manage on their own. It also mitigates some of the challenges that a distributed innovation culture can pose to those less-inclined to innovate. However, the tendency of committees to "manage" innovation and stifle creative efforts is a potential threat that must be considered.

There is no optimal answer to the innovation model conundrum as every legal business is different. However, the Kodak example shows that it is crucial to ensure that the model you choose works with your organization's existing business context and that it facilitates good and flexible strategic decision-making around innovation.

Maximizing your leadership model – developing an innovation strategy

Establishing the right person, or group of people, to lead innovation is crucial to the development and implementation of innovation efforts. Innovation is capable of taking an organization down a number of different roads, but embarking on an innovation program without some sense of direction might end up getting you very lost. The "move fast and break things" attitude advocated by firms such as Facebook can actually cause chaos, uncertainty, and failure. Not only does this approach not gain traction within the legal industry's traditionally risk averse environment, but it can also facilitate poor strategic choices.

A good innovation strategy should not cause chaos, nor should it create bureaucracy or stifle creativity. A well-planned innovation strategy should be flexible enough to allow you to react to the ever-changing legal market conditions quickly by providing information about your organization's current strengths, weaknesses, opportunities and threats – and by defining the priority areas that the organization wants to focus on. This clear strategy should also ensure that, no matter what leadership model you have adopted for innovation, your leadership can take good decisions about investments that may have uncertain returns in the short term, but that have the potential to drive the organization's longer term strategic vision.

Positioning – where are you now?

Planning an innovation strategy can follow a similar structure to traditional business strategy planning, and indeed, it should complement your traditional business strategy. Johnson, Whittington, Scholes, Angwin & Regner's strategic planning model identifies strategic positioning as a core element of any planning exercise, and the same is true of any innovation strategy process. Innovation is a journey, and as with any journey, it is important to know your starting point before you

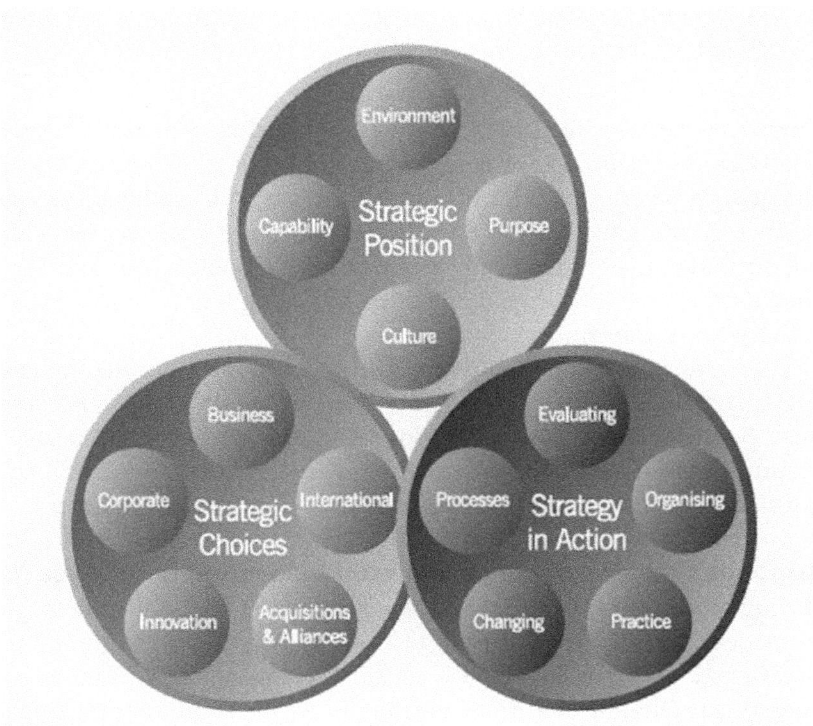

Figure 1: Strategic planning model.
Source: Johnson, Whittington, Scholes, Angwin & Regner (2013).[3]

embark. Familiarizing yourself with where you are now in relation to your environment, capability, purpose, and culture can help you plan and prioritize your strategic choices about where you want innovation to take you, and your plan for how you are going to get there.

You can determine your own position by asking several questions in relation to five key areas:

1. **Clients.** Who are your clients, what are you famous for with them, and what unfulfilled needs do they have?
2. **Competitors**. Who are your competitors, what are they good at, and what are they doing to innovate?
3. **People**. Who are your people, what do they value about your organization's culture, and how are they approaching innovation?
4. **Capabilities**. What skills and capabilities do you have access to, and what gaps do you have?
5. **Environment**. What is happening in the environment you operate in, at both a macro-economic level and an industry level?

There are several strategic planning tools that can help you answer these questions in a structured way and, once you have those answers, you should have a very good idea of your current strengths and weaknesses as an organization. You should also have a lead on some high-level opportunities that might benefit from creative approaches, and you should have a sense of some of the threats you might need to find innovative ways of combating.

Of course, innovation should be a fluid and agile exercise, and there is a danger that too much navel gazing will inhibit you from the important business of just going out and making things happen. This is a concern that needs to be balanced, and you need to ensure that you do not get lost in the planning and forget to go out and make innovation happen.

Strategic choices – where do you want innovation to take you?

Having taken the time to understand your starting point for your innovation journey, the next step is to identify where you want your efforts to take you, and crucially, to also consider where you don't want to go as an organization so that you can stop the organization from pursuing fruitless opportunities.

Perhaps, for you, innovation is about differentiating yourself from your competitors and you want to focus the majority of your efforts on disruptive and risky innovations that lead the market. Or perhaps you would rather reduce your risk by being a fast-follower who can learn from others' mistakes.

Conversely, you may want to use innovation as a way of becoming a cost-leader in your area of the market and therefore you will focus on small wins that optimize your current product offering, and/or those that help you develop other cost-effective products and services.

Alternatively, your strategy may be to focus on cooperating with others on innovative solutions. Or, you may also choose to use innovation to help you enter new markets, geographies, products or service lines. It may even be some combination of each of these, or something else entirely.

No matter what choices you make, and what choices you choose deliberately not to pursue, your ultimate strategy should be inspirational, aspirational, and forward-looking. If it feels safe and achievable then you probably aren't doing enough – though once again, balance is key and it should not be too whimsical, as it needs to take account of the realities of your actual environment, particularly in relation to how readily you can access resource and investment. A purely aspirational strategy that will never be achieved is of no use to anyone.

To that end, your innovation strategy should also not gather dust on a shelf but should be agile and adaptive, evolving to keep pace with your changing environment. It needs to enable you to monitor your environment, innovate constantly, and to change your leadership model or your strategy if you need to.

Conclusion

No matter what model you choose, no matter what strategy you select for your organization, innovation is a buzzword that is unlikely to go away any time soon. But to deliver it requires strong leadership who are able to provide sustainable and strategic innovation. Each organization needs to take the time to choose the right leadership model to suit their culture and business model, and to develop their strategic approach to innovation in order to ensure that they don't miss opportunities to capture truly transformative ideas.

This chapter originally appeared in *Strategic Innovation as an Emerging Firm Function*, published in October 2018.

References

1. McAlone, Nathan. "This man invented the digital camera in 1975 – and his bosses at Kodak never let it see the light of day." *UK Business Insider.* August 17, 2015. http://uk.businessinsider.com/this-man-invented-the-digital-camera-in-1975-and-his-bosses-at-kodak-never-let-it-see-the-light-of-day-2015-8
2. Anthony, Scott. "Kodak's downfall wasn't about technology." *Harvard Business Review.* June 2016. https://hbr.org/2016/07/kodaks-downfall-wasnt-about-technology
3. Johnson, G., Scholes, K., & Whittington, R. (2008). *Exploring corporate strategy: text & cases.* Pearson education.

Chapter 11:
Why innovate? The link between strategy and innovation

By Langdon Morris, InnovationLabs LLC, USA

When the publishers of this book first contacted me and inquired as to whether I might be interested in writing a chapter, I had to pause for a moment and think about it. I'm not an attorney, after all, but I do know a little about strategy and innovation. And then my thinking shifted and I realized that the work we do with our clients, primarily advising them on strategy and innovation, nearly always has significant legal implications. Which made me realize, of course, that I did indeed want to write this chapter, because it's a great topic and I welcomed the opportunity to explore it with you.

So where to begin? First, a word about the relationship between innovation and strategy in a general way. It's a close relationship, because innovation efforts, the most useful and value-creating ones, are undertaken *in service to* strategy. That is, the purpose of innovation is to make an organization more fit to its competitive environment, more capable of surviving and thriving. Fitness for survival is one of the most important strategic themes imaginable, and that's what strategy is all about, so this tells us that to innovate effectively we have to know what our strategic goals are, as this defines the landscape in which we need to be searching and developing.

We can frame the issue in the inverse as well. There's no point in developing innovations that do not address the firm's strategic goals, as this would clearly be a waste of time, money, and expertise. No, we want to focus on the areas in which we can make the most difference, and add the most value to the long-term viability of the firm. Consequently, prospective innovators have to be fully conversant with a firm's strategy so that they can steer their efforts appropriately.

This brings up a second important question, which is, "Who is it that's doing the innovating?" In an auto company, like Toyota, the answer is that everyone is. Toyota is world-renowned as the number one manufacturing firm, and one of the main reasons for its success is that it has successfully engaged the entire organization in thinking about innovation for decade after decade. Indeed, one of the greatest management books of all time is *40 YEARS, 20 MILLION IDEAS: The Toyota Suggest System*, by Yuzo Yasuda. The title says it all. This is how you become world-class in innovation, when you make cars.

World class innovation

But how do you become world class at innovation when you are a professional services firm, like, say, a law firm? Firms that bill hourly like to have their people doing hourly-billable work, so is that different? Maybe, but not really. Toyota people design and build cars, but in the daily course of doing so they have ideas, just like people reviewing deals, preparing and defending suits, and writing contracts. So let's create a system to capture those ideas.

And what are those ideas likely to be about? Some will be internal suggestions, such as, "We should do such-and-such differently, like this, and it would be easier and better". And, "Could we get better coffee in the canteen, please?" And, "We should try that new AI contract-writing tool and see if it can help us get through this massive workload we have over the next three months with client x".

Wait, what? AIs can review (and presumably) write contracts? Oh, this is changing the game, as now law firms have a new kind of competition. That's different. Yes, we really do need to think differently about strategy and innovation if we're going to be competing with robots.

And yes, we all realize that technology is advancing very quickly, and that it's changing nearly everything about how we live and work, how we entertain ourselves and interact, and what we think, feel, believe, and expect. In fact, it's changing the entire character of society as well as the structure of the global economy, and not just in small and simple ways, but in profound and enduring ones.

What we're experiencing is disruption, a classic case of it perhaps from the perspective of economic history, but a very challenging experience when you're living it day to day, and trying to figure out what your own firm should do to survive and thrive. If you're a strategy or innovation officer in a law firm, how long has that title even existed in your profession? For how long have lawyers been thinking about how they should bring innovation into their practices? Well, it's a good thing to be thinking about now.

Just as all types of businesses in all sectors of the economy are having to adapt to these changes, law firms are no different. Let's consider some examples. When companies started offshoring their IT processing to India, did lawyers anticipate that legal work would follow in its footsteps? When hospitals started sending x-rays to India to be analyzed, did lawyers realize that they'd soon be drafting contracts with the help of robots? When the Oil Shock of 1974 hit, did the American auto companies foresee it as the beginning of their downfall and the rise of Japanese, quality-focused manufacturing? Not right away, but within a few years they woke up. What happened in 2000 when the founders of Netflix offered to sell their company to the at-the-time market leader Blockbuster Video? The Blockbuster executives laughed. But they were not laughing a few years later when Blockbuster went bankrupt and Netflix was worth billions. And what happened at Nokia when Apple introduced the iPhone in 2007? They also laughed. Foolishly.

And on that tremulous first day of classes when the law school class of 2014 began their studies in the fall of 2011, did they realize that more than 40 percent of them would struggle to find employment for more than a year after they passed the bar? Of course not. Or a good many of them would never have decided to put themselves so deeply in debt in the first place.

A time of change

So now we have artificial intelligence (robots, essentially) drafting and reviewing contracts. Legal-bots. And we have AIs driving cars (and occasionally killing people too). Amazon has 50,000 robots (more by the time you read this, actually) working in its warehouses, and DJ.com is delivering products to 100 villages in China using drones. And there's a fast food restaurant that was recently spun out of MIT that uses only robots in its kitchens. So no coffee breaks, no cut fingers, no sick days, just work, work, work.

Everything is changing, which makes it a fascinating time to be in law. After all, how long is it going to take to work out the statutory structures to manage the liabilities associated with self-driving cars, drones, and robot warehouse workers? There will be accidents and injuries and deaths, and legal liabilities associated with all of it. Different nations, and different states and provinces within them, will write and pass differing laws, and the firms that can cope with the burgeoning complexity of all this will certainly have significant advantages in the coming years.

Let's go back to the Oil Shock of 1974 example. The auto makers that caught on to the new market demands first, and took advantage of the situation by bringing high quality and good gas mileage cars to the market, were the ones that gained market share from the new market conditions.

Those that didn't... didn't. Of course it wasn't just auto firms that were affected. Oil firms were massively affected as well. In 1970 there were seven major global oil firms, collectively known as the Seven Sisters. Shell was the weakest of the seven when the Oil Shock hit, which occurred when the oil producing nations formed the OPEC cartel and seized control of oil production, primarily across the Middle East. Shell, however, was the first to grasp the strategic implications of OPEC, and the company started making strategic moves according to the new rules of the game. Consequently, by 1980 Shell had become the strongest of the sisters.

So the same will be true for law firms in today's rapidly changing conditions. Those who recognize the new rules, the new competitive structure, and who act accordingly and well, will gain significant advantage.

What other factors are going to be changing the competitive structure in the coming years?

I mentioned AI and autonomous, mobile devices already. To that, add connected devices. Soon every device will be talking to every other device in a realm known in tech circles as "the device mesh", or more simply, IoT, Internet of Things. Some credible analysts are forecasting that by 2025 we may see 500 million robots, and 500 *billion* connected devices in use worldwide. Those are staggering numbers, the consequences of which will be enormous. All aspects of work will be transformed, as humans are displaced in massive numbers by robots, including lawyers. However, the legal work required to get all this in place will be equally staggering, which reminds us that one of the most important roles for the strategist/innovator in your firm is to figure out how your firm should play, or not play, in these markets.

Who are your key clients, and what aspects of automation and AI are going to be the most legally significant to them in the coming years? And how can your firm develop the necessary skills and expertise?

The impact of technology

Another emerging field of law that will be coming along a little more gradually, but surely nonetheless, pertains to the legal rights of the robots themselves. Yes, it's coming. Presently, science cannot offer us a definition of "consciousness", but we're moving quickly toward the time when machines will be conscious in some moderately-recognizable way, at which point a robot will sue for its legal rights, and the whole regime of civil law will change. Gradually, but it will change. What rights and obligations do robots have, and what obligations do humans have with respect to the robots they own? Will it even be legitimate for people to "own" robots, if those robots have consciousness and human-grade intelligence?

Yes, of course you may be chuckling about the far-fetched nature of this today, but not for long. Threats and opportunities are fully intertwined. Who got the first calls when a Tesla car killed its owner? After the police and the family, next came the lawyers.

We're about to be surrounded with technologies for which entirely new areas of law are going to have to be developed, case by case, suit by suit, appeal by appeal. Robotics law, self-driving-vehicle law, drone law, clone law, CRISPR law....

Suppose someone's grandmother dies because a robot forgets to administer her heart medication? The robot maker, or the software coders they subcontracted the work to? But did the code get hacked? Did you know that hackers recently took remote control of a self-driving car while it was driving? Why? Just to show the car company (Chrysler) that they could – a warning.

Does your firm work in finance? What's the impact of blockchain going to be? Don't know? That's because no one knows. It could be a flash in the pan, or it could transform everything about money and trade. It could be hype-squared, or disruption-cubed. If you're the strategist/innovator in a law firm that deals anywhere in finance, insurance, or trade, you'll have to know.

Have you heard of "smart contracts"? These are blockchain-based agreements in which real-world events trigger actions automatically. Wrapped up in these contracts and blockchains are concepts including trust, identity, verification, and validation, none of which are simple or trivial.

For example, the UN is working on a blockchain-based identity system for the millions of people currently living in refugee camps. Their nation-state is no longer able to provide proper identity documents for them, so they're trapped within the barbed wire fences until someone can create a passport for them that attests to their identity in a manner that authorities in other nations will accept.

Speaking of nations, the blockchain is also fostering the concept of "self-sovereignty", which is a movement to get away from the necessity of having an external authority such as the nation attest to who you are. Think about the elements of your identity and how they're scattered around the world like leaves blown in the wind. If you're an American, here's what it might look like. Your Social Security number was issued by the Social Security Administration. Your passport was issued by the State Department. Your driver's license comes from the State where you live.

Your birth certificate was issued by a hospital and then officially recorded in the city or county where you were born. Your credit report (which has been hacked, by the way) is in three databases owned by private companies. You do business on dozens of websites, each of which has its own password scheme. Some of them store lots of information about you, like Facebook and Google do, and sell that information to advertisers who want to influence your purchases (and votes). You have three credit cards (what, more than three?), a few bank accounts, and a charge card for gas, each of which is another account with another institution. You have a mortgage, which you bought from a mortgage lender but which has since been sold three times and now you make payments to some entity that you don't even know. And you rely on *all* of these institutions to attest to who you say you are at various times, like when you want to buy a car, or another house, or travel to another country, or when you get stopped for speeding. Yes, your identity is scattered hither and yon. You are a subject, not a sovereign.

But with the blockchain it might not have to be. If the reality lives up to the promised hype, then within a few years you could start moving off the grid without becoming a survivalist. For which, of course, there are extensive legal implications, and who better but your own firm to become the world's leading expert in the new fields of "identity law", "cryptocurrency law", and "automaton-liability law".

Don't forget about "climate change law", because who's going to pay whom when Miami is flooded under 20 feet of water and the multi-million dollar beachfront condos are accessible only by boat because the beach is gone? What about "space law"? Someone's going to start mining on the moon pretty soon, and then what? A clone attacked me… do I sue the clone, or the cloned, or the cloner?

Choosing a strategic direction

If you choose one or more of these as a strategic direction for your firm, you will have to then engage in innovating. You will invest in learning, some prototypes, maybe some partnerships with tech or blockchain firms you can work with. You'll hire a new grad or two who specialized in technology law in school, maybe someone from Stanford who also took classes at Stanford's D. school and learned how world class innovators do it.

So you get the picture, right? Technology is driving change, and change means new areas of law have to be developed. And this is all occurring as the legal profession itself is being subjected to threats from technology also. Fascinating times, these.

Ok, a short recap. The *purpose* of innovation is to enable firms to survive and thrive under changing conditions. And boy, are things changing these days. To be an *effective* innovator you have to be clear about what your strategic direction is (and is not), and then you have to direct innovation efforts towards the most promising targets. What those innovations will be you cannot know in advance, so you have to invest in learning and discovery first. (If you knew, it wouldn't be "innovation", it would be "development".)

The notion that innovation can be directed is important, because random innovation efforts always fail. We can say to people, "We're really interested in thoughts and ideas in (these) directions", and be specific about what "these" are. There will naturally still be ideas that come up outside of the preferred directions, and they may well be valuable, and we welcome them. But we want to steer 60 to 80 percent of the innovation efforts in preferred directions.

Innovation in this way is an extended conversation, and one of the key reasons that law firms can benefit from having a strategy or innovation leader among their partners is that they are the ones who can both steer those conversations, and also initiate them. This is *proactive innovation*, a very worthwhile thing to do. It doesn't have to take a lot of time, because even only a few hours of informed brainstorming can really open people's eyes, and lead to all kinds of interesting and worthwhile possibilities.

And why do this now? Because, given the rapid advances of technology and the transformation it is causing to the economy, the consequences for the legal profession are fundamental. Systematic innovation effort by all law firms is necessary in order to avoid becoming, well, let's just say completely superfluous in the market. In many industries the choice is already "innovate or die", and this choice is coming soon to the legal profession as well.

So get clear on what your strategy is, and then channel your firm's significant brainpower toward innovations that address strategic goals and imperatives. That's the link.

This chapter originally appeared in *Strategic Innovation as an Emerging Firm Function*, published in October 2018.

Chapter 12:
The fundamental challenges facing any new or future leader

By Patrick J McKenna, internationally recognized author, lecturer, strategist, and advisor

Being any kind of leader within a law firm should come with a clear warning: this job could seriously change you and how you behave within your firm!

Over the past decade I have had the privilege – through my consulting, research, and interviews – to peek behind the veil surrounding the challenge of becoming a *new* managing partner (or whatever title best signifies your firm's leader). From candid discussions about the stress involved in looking like you know what you are doing and the huge time demands imposed by your partner's requests, to feeling disorientated by the scale and scope of the mandate, many professionals quietly struggle with the various pressures that accompany their term in office. I discovered that the great majority of leaders, in any position of responsibility, are at their most vulnerable early in their tenure.

As a new or future leader, you may be surprised to feel confused and indecisive just at the time you want to appear clear-sighted and strong-minded. You may feel overwhelmed and anxious just when you would far rather be seen as composed and dynamic. In fact, what I've discerned is that there are a number of challenging leadership questions – the more or less ongoing dynamics of the role that incumbents wrestle with to effectively handle the job of being a leader.

Here are the top five:

- Do I shake things up or do I preserve the status quo?
- Do I strengthen my bonds with people or do I maintain a distance?
- Do I demonstrate that I know what to do or do I ask for help?
- Do I strongly influence the decision I want or do I facilitate a consensus?
- Do I focus on achieving results or do I accept a degree of uncertainty?

Each of us, when serving as a leader, has a natural predilection to favor one approach or the other, to gravitate to one extremity over the other. Our preference, therefore, as to whether to "shake things up" or to "preserve the status quo" is often hard-wired into us, the result of past experience gained *before* entering into our current leadership position. What seasoned leaders come to learn is that the only way to navigate these tensions successfully is to try to manage both ends simultaneously.

Let's take a look at these five with an eye toward what you, as a new or future leader, might do to navigate them. To give you a sense of what it truly feels like on the front lines, each of the following sections leads off with a quotation from a real-life law firm leader (kept anonymous for reasons that will become apparent).

Do I shake things up or preserve the status quo?

> *Lawyers are creatures of habit and busy lawyers even more so – the time and effort to "condition" them to new modes of operating should not be underestimated. On a variety of change initiatives, my personal goal is to reduce the time from "that's the dumbest idea I ever heard" to "we always do it that way" from five years to three years!*

Your first area of tension as a leader is to obtain some sense of agreement from your partners on the direction your firm, office, or practice group should pursue. That direction has a great deal to do with the performance you as the leader are charged to deliver. It also has a great deal to do with your partners' collective appetite for change. "Our dilemma," explained one managing partner, "is that we hate change and love it at the same time. What my partners want is for things to remain the same but get better."

There are many questions that you could probably utilize with partners to get a grip on the direction your partners want to go, but two are pivotal:

- What are the critical things we need to change as a firm and why?
- What are the most important things about our law firm that we should be sure to preserve and why?

As early as possible as a leader, you must get your partners' input into what they see as the group's preferable direction. Conduct one-on-one interview sessions with your partners – asking each one the same questions to get their insights, solicit their advice, and see what themes emerge. Clarify what they want to see you "shake up" and what they want to see you "preserve". It is wise to have your partners see that you are genuinely engaged and willing to listen before you ever speak about where you think the firm needs to go.

Your interview goals:

- Absorb information from your partners;
- Define or confirm the firm's key challenges;
- Establish credibility and win trust;
- Assess your partners' appetite for change; and
- Gather input for developing your strategic agenda for going forward.

Doing nothing but listening, for as long as you can stand it, is the most important thing you can do.

Ask yourself: how do I begin to make a difference? What do I want to make a difference about? Regrettably, some leaders accept unachievable missions and targets that are far too ambitious, while others are told little about what is expected other than "continue to make improvements". If you believe that the direction you are being asked to undertake is not achievable or able to be accomplished within the timeframe expected, make your feelings known as early as possible in your tenure.

Do I strengthen my bonds with people or maintain a distance?

> *I realized that fundamentally my relations with my partners would never be the same. Everyone has an agenda when they talk to you. As managing partner, you become more isolated and can never again just be "one of the guys".*

In what circumstances will people follow you as a leader? Usually, for people to follow they need to have a strong relationship with you; they need to feel that they know you as a human being; and they need to feel a connection and sense of empathy for your beliefs, values, and stated priorities. Concurrently, these very same partners need to feel that you have invested the time to really know and understand them, and have a solid grasp on what they value and hold important.

Without a strong sense of relationship between you and your colleagues, great goals are impossible to set, performance cannot be sustained, major difficulties cannot be overcome, and new opportunities rarely get created.

Alternatively there is also the danger that when a leader tends to lose their independence from their colleagues, they can tend to get identified with one cliché or coalition in the firm. At one firm recently we overhead one of the partners commenting that a particular proposition, while rather absurd, would likely get positive attention, only because the originator was a FOG. When we naively asked what a FOG was, the partner responded: "Oh, that is an acronym for Friend Of Greg" – the firm's chairman and managing partner.

However, tension is generated if you emphasize keeping your distance from colleagues, as you may create a sense of aloofness, potential mistrust, and encounter resistance when you try to get things accomplished. You may soon detect increased feelings of division within the firm.

Your partners are not interested in your title. They want to know if you care about them as a person, if you care about helping them solve their problems and enhancing their careers. Consider building and maintaining relationships as a critical part of your leadership role. Remember that leading is always done *with* others, not *to* them. Everyone wants a cheerleader, someone to believe in them, to help them have a can-do attitude. What can you do to let every partner know that you believe they can become even more of a success?

As a leader, you will be under a microscope, being observed (your decisions, how you make them, whom you consult with) very carefully (what you say and the signals you send). You will be barraged with phone calls and emails – with questions, requests, and advice. You may need some time to transform some relationships. Good leaders customize the relationship created to each individual.

Do I give the appearance that I know what I'm doing or ask for help?

Not withstanding all of the qualities I believe I have, I'm feeling like I'm a fish out of water. Yet how do I tell anyone what I'm going through? I need them to go on believing in me and trusting that I know what I'm doing.

When you are new to the function and responsibility of managing and leading the entire firm, you are starting out with an enormous amount to learn. You soon find that the skills that made you a highly successful practitioner are not necessarily the same skills that will now transform you into a successful leader.

If you come across to your partners as having all the answers, knowing what to do, and showing everyone how to succeed, you risk being seen as imposing your views, being uninterested in the opinions of other partners, and prone to antagonizing and irritating those same partners.

Alternatively, if you are perceived to overdo the "seek help" side of the spectrum, you may then risk being seen as lightweight and unsubstantial. Partners may soon wonder if you are ever going to get around to adding any value.

The tension therefore arises as you realize that you should not come across as a "know-it-all". However, at the other end of this spectrum, your people will not be confident in the direction that the firm is taking unless you act as though you know precisely where the firm should be going, what it will encounter along the way, and what the destination will look like once it has been reached.

Heed the old adage: "He who asks a question is a fool for five minutes, but he who doesn't is a fool for the rest of their life". Most people want the leader to succeed and will be willing to help you learn so that you can add value.

All learning challenges a person's self-image. As a leader, you need to recognize that learning will mean that you will have to modify some of your viewpoints and certainties.

You will function more effectively when you have a confidant – someone that you can trust and confer with, who understands the joys and successes, the difficulties and frustrations of leadership.

Do I push for the decision I want or facilitate a shared consensus?

> *In some cases I've learned that I need to be more explicit … "there is where I believe we need to be going and this is what I think we need to do to get there, based on the discussions that I've had".*

Deciding who will make what decisions and how decisions will be reached is a fundamental leadership act.

On the one hand, you know that your partners will likely take more responsibility for implementing decisions that they themselves have played a part in making. This argues for wider distribution and a consensus decision-making style.

On the other hand, you know that you must often reconcile the conflicting interests of appealing to partners who don't want to move too quickly with the market reality that opportunity windows don't stay open forever. This argues for a quicker decision than obtaining full consensus might allow. Whether to influence or facilitate can be a function of firm culture, leader personality, and situational dynamics. It definitely shapes how your firm will operate.

Things can get very stuck with this tension. Of all the tensions noted, you may very well tend to identify most strongly with either influencing or facilitating as your preferred style. Research shows that what we are skilled at is what tends to get reinforced. As a firm leader you will confront more complex situations than you may be used to and more complex than your habits are suited for. If you stick rigidly to only one (influence or facilitate) way of handling the situation you may become far less effective as a leader than someone who works at developing their skills in both of these decision-making formats. What is required, as with the other tensions, is an appropriate dosage of both influencing and facilitating.

Do I focus on results above all else or accept a degree of uncertainty?

You don't want to show any weakness, any self-doubt, any concern about making a difficult decision. Remember, you are the firm leader, which means nothing but confidence and high energy when you walk into a room.

As a leader, you are likely to want to achieve some impressive results during your tenure. You will go to considerable lengths to achieve those results, since your sense of self-worth, personal reputation, and ultimately, your leadership legacy depends on producing measurable results.

Your challenge is that you inhabit a world infused with uncertainty. So simply being methodical and persevering will not necessarily guarantee that you get the results you want. As a leader, you need to have the ability to be comfortable with uncertainty, to live with it, and not to be fazed by it.

You don't have to like living with a sense of uncertainty, but you must anticipate new developments, recognize trends, and understand change. As a leader, you must stay on top of information about the trends affecting the profession and your various business opportunities. Your future is directly linked to your ability to respond quickly and with flexibility.

Leadership is about credibility. Credibility requires confidence, certainty and capability. Allowing others to see that you lack certainty can be dangerous in the real world. Once doubts about the leader's certainty begin to form, they can be very difficult to repair. Every leader knows this and fears it.

It is very human to stay with doing what is comfortable. Make a conscious effort to turn off the old tapes that are playing in your mind and be willing to let go of the past. The most effective way to minimize the intimidating effect of uncertainty is through planning. The more understanding you have of the likely-to-happen event, the less debilitating the change will be.

Knowing when to unlock from a declared position and advocate a new one calls for courage. Accept that you will not be 100 percent right in all of your judgment calls. Beware of the mindset imposed by your professional training and your ego's need to be right. If any of your decisions turn out to be wrong, and they will, don't confuse the business need to change direction with feeling that you are looking indecisive.

Keep learning as you go

Transforming into a leader is no small challenge. It is very human to get discouraged at times. Sometimes others will criticize your objectives. Sometimes attaining your goals will seem harder than you thought. Just remember that there is always an element of personal sacrifice and a need to remain flexible when one undertakes a leadership role. When challenges arise or unexpected events occur, the value of a leader with a high-faith factor cannot be underestimated. It is a powerful motivator for every individual you lead.

All successful leaders work through these five challenges over some time during their incumbency. I believe that taking the time to think through these issues at the *start* of your tenure will give you a more informed basis for formulating your objectives and pursuing your goals.

Addendum – where new leaders spend their time

In accepting any new leadership position you are dealing with *firsts*. And as with other firsts in life, where specifically you choose to invest your precious and finite leadership time can impact your future effectiveness and leave a long-lasting impression on everyone involved. It goes without saying, therefore, that where you spend your time should be entered into with some thoughtful and deliberate intent.

In an attempt to examine where new leaders have spent their time, I surveyed and spoke with the new managing partners of 19 US law firms, between 100 and over 500 attorneys in size. My objective was to determine specifically whether there were any identifiable patterns for where these leaders spent their time, how productive they viewed their initial efforts, and now in hindsight, whether there was anything they might have done differently.

I started by inviting each of them to identify three key activities that consumed the better part of their time during their first few months in the role. Many of them lamented that they were "much more internally focused than externally during this period" and 24 percent of the respondents cited their efforts to proactively contact, meet with and interview fellow partners/shareholders as the primary activity that consumed the greatest portion of their management time.

While that may have been the deliberate objective of a good number of these new leaders, another 18 percent found themselves busy responding to their partners' requests for meetings and assistance with various matters while another 18 percent found themselves actively participating in the annual partner review, appraisal, and compensation process – usually as a result of them having taken up their new position in January.

Question 1:

"Looking back to the period following the announcement of you becoming the firm's new leader and the first 100 days or so of your term, which three activities consumed the greatest portion of your management time?"

Responses in order to magnitude of time spent:

1. Contacting, meeting, and interviewing my fellow partners (24 percent);
2. Responding to my partners' various requests for assistance/meetings (18 percent);
3. Participating in annual partner review, appraisal, and compensation (18 percent);
4. Beginning to reshape the firm's strategy (16 percent);
5. Assessing, rearranging, and replacing members of my internal admin team (eight percent);
6. Learning and better understanding the financial aspects of the firm (five percent);
7. Attending practice group meetings to learn what each group is doing (five percent);
8. Meeting with associates and staff (two percent);
9. Understanding the trends and competitive dynamics of the marketplace (two percent);

10. Reading through meeting minutes and other materials (zero percent);
11. Participating in development of firm's annul budget (zero percent); and
12. Making contact and meeting with the firm's key clients (zero percent).

The results above were encapsulated by one respondent who told us, "*I didn't appreciate the amount of time I would spend in meetings... meetings with administrative staff and meetings with attorneys. People want to be heard.*"

And from another managing partner, I heard, "*The care and feeding of your law partners is a challenge. Each partner is unique and I never know what (seemingly minor) issue will bring out passion, anger and/or terror in a fellow partner.*"

In addition to the 12 activities listed above, a few respondents cited specific projects that they were committed to working on during their first few months. These leaders identified such things as opening a new office, re-establishing their firm's role and visibility within the community, implementing a new compensation policy, working with partners on accounts receivable, and establishing more support for the attorneys' business development efforts.

There was one particular activity that provoked some mixed feelings and that was whether a new firm leader should be involved, immediately upon taking office, in participating in the partners' annual reviews.

"*Our normal compensation review for our partners consumes most of February,*" commented the new presiding partner of one firm. Some felt that the time required was brutal and others commented that this was not an ideal way to have to interact with their peers as the firm's new leader.

On a related note, some were consumed with internal personnel issues that they wished their predecessor would have handled.

"*The internal issues actually started before my term began, when I was 'shadowing' my predecessor. It turns out that we really have some average, as opposed to stellar performance. I will be replacing our COO and probably others. This should not have been 'my problem,' but it is what it is.*"

Applying hindsight

After having heard where leaders actually invested (proactively or reactively) their initial management time, I then posed the question of whether that was the right area to focus on.

Question 2:

"Looking back to the period following the announcement of you becoming the firm's new leader and the first 100 days or so of your term, do you think the amount of time spent on each of these activities should have been lower or higher?"

I should have spent MORE time on:

- Making contact and meeting with the firm's key clients (28 percent);
- Attending practice group meetings to learn what each group was doing (17 percent);
- Contacting, meeting and interviewing my fellow partners (14 percent); and
- Learning and better understanding the financial aspects of the firm (11 percent).

I should have spent LESS time on:

- Responding to my partners' various requests for assistance/ meetings (45 percent);
- Reading through meeting minutes and other materials (18 percent); and
- Participating in annual partner review, appraisal, and compensation (nine percent).

When asked whether, with the benefit of hindsight, they should have prioritized differently, respondents said that they would have focused more time in a number of areas. Interestingly, the most common refrain (from 28 percent) was, "*I should have spent more time with clients.*"

And in spite of "interviewing partners" having been cited as the highest rated time consumer, another 31 percent of firm leaders emphasized the need to spend far more time communicating with partners, either in practice groups or one-on-one. "*I can never communicate enough with my partners, even though I have been trying very hard in this regard,*" explained one firm chair.

The one area in which firm leaders regret spending so much of their time was with responding to "*every minor and trivial partner request and sitting in on meetings that seemed to make little sense for me to ever attend.*"

In the words of one DC managing partner:

"Time passes so very quickly in this position. There is so much to do and so little time to do it. My biggest challenge has been tending to my personal practice while still giving enough time to management issues. There is NOT enough time to do both. While I work on one for a few days, the other suffers. Simply reading all of my email is a challenge. Also, each day seems to pass very quickly without me being able to pinpoint what I accomplished. It is difficult to move forward my major initiatives without doing it on weekends."

And from one West Coast firm leader:

"I really feel that I should be spending more time on all these issues. That, of course, is not possible. I do just enough to keep all of the balls moving forward. What I really need to do more of is 'management by walking around'."

Leadership tensions

My final question of these managing partners was intended to reflect another important element of the first 100 days – the need for any new leader to balance the various tensions that may emerge. I was curious to discover whether there were any particular tensions that surfaced more often than others during these initial months.

While the responses I received were all across the board, one particular leader expressed the thought that one could probably summarize my entire list of 14 tensions into his "*needing to galvanize the partners to take ownership of the firm's issues and to act like equity partners*".

In this managing partner's words:

"Generally speaking, I enjoyed the first 100 days. In many respects it was less frustrating and more satisfying to implement your own judgment since a new managing partner is given deference, rather than having to work hard to influence others and work behind the scenes. Patience is definitely a virtue in this job but at the same time I need, and people have responded to, the bully pulpit to exhort the partners to act outside their professional 'billing attorney' box."

Question 3:

"Looking back to the period following the announcement of you becoming the firm's new leader and the first 100 days or so of your term, which three of the following normal leadership tensions would you say were the most challenging for you?"

- Being patient while becoming productive – 13 percent;
- Setting your own pace while following the firm's pace – eight percent;
- Trusting your intuition while making deliberate decisions – eight percent;
- Pleasing your partners while ensuring you meet your own priorities – 15 percent;
- Initiating change while respecting the history and culture of the firm – 13 percent;
- Demonstrating competence while seeking advice when needed – three percent;
- Building new relationships while resting assumptions about others – five percent;
- Taking appropriate action while waiting for enough information – five percent;
- Drawing on past experience while not letting past experience blind you to new realities – three percent;
- Acting with conviction while being open to learning – three percent;
- Influencing decisions while facilitating a consensus – ten percent;
- Not leading with your ego while displaying confidence – five percent;
- Making your position clear while seeking input and feedback – eight percent; and
- Strengthening bonds while maintaining professional boundaries with people – three percent.

As you can see, the top three tensions that seemed to resonate with most new leaders were:

1. Pleasing your partners while ensuring that you meet your own priorities;
2. Being patient while becoming productive; and
3. Initiating change while respecting the history and culture of the firm.

It goes without saying that an important element of the first 100 days is the need for the new managing partner to establish respect in his leadership role at the top. As one respondent expressed it to me at the end of our discussion, "*I see my job as maximizing credibility with my partners while moving forward with the least amount of dislocation*".

A version of this chapter originally appeared in *Legal Leadership: a Handbook for Future Success*, published in November 2018.

Part five: Horizon scanning

Chapter 13: The inevitability of multi-disciplinary practices

By Michael Roster, formerly GC of Stanford University and formerly managing partner of Morrison & Foerster's Los Angeles office

Much has been written about how lawyers are being replaced by artificial intelligence and new types of service providers, accounting firms are absorbing and replacing law firms, and mergers into worldwide megafirms of 3,000 to 10,000 lawyers is the only way to survive. Steve Jobs and others have called the process "creative destruction". Richard Susskind referred to it years ago as the end of lawyers.

I believe these are merely symptoms and, in most cases, wrong responses to what is happening: *the disaggregation of what lawyers traditionally have done*. Over time, in my view and with some exceptions, lawyers and their law firms will be replaced with highly efficient multi-disciplinary practices (MDPs) that offer bundled services and yield measurably better outcomes at a fraction of current costs.

If done right, MDPs will also be far more satisfying places to work, although lawyers may find they play significantly diminished roles, whether as outside or in-house counsel. As part of the transformation, the chief legal officer/general counsel will often be replaced by a newly created position of chief risk/compliance/solutions officer, who sometimes will be a lawyer, sometimes not.

In my opinion, the accounting firms won't be the right platform. They are too big, rigid and, given their audit culture, process-oriented rather than outcomes-oriented. In addition, they will need to be split up still once again because of regulatory and company requirements for independent auditors.

Law firms largely won't be the winners either. Lawyers typically aren't good managers. Our training is to identify issues (the "what if" part of what we do) but only a small set of really good lawyers are also good at the other half of the equation, which is "so what". That is, lawyers who have the expertise and confidence to decide what really matters and then to advise a client what actually to do. The megafirms will be especially inefficient given their high overhead and income expectations versus the more granular pricing that is needed for diverse practice groups to be competitive.

Layered on top of all of this will be the problem of conflicts. The efficient provider of multi-disciplinary services will serve hundreds of entities in the same lines of business; those entities may have similar issues but also periodically may sue one another, as well as do deals with one another. As a former general counsel of a major university and medical center and then a nationwide financial services company, I never had a problem with a law firm representing my competitors in compliance and similar matters. I knew from my own days as a law firm partner that these firms would have greater expertise and reliability because they handle hundreds of similar matters and clients. My senior management was fine with that as well. What my fellow executives and board members couldn't accept was that a law firm with which we had shared highly sensitive information might periodically be on the other side, suing us. And what many law firm leaders don't seem to realize is, this doesn't turn simply on bar association rules of ethics. It's the appearance of it that impacts a company's senior managers.

Finally, most MDP work will be performed by highly skilled professionals who aren't lawyers. They will see no benefit in being housed in the large accounting and law firms that impose procedures that undermine efficiency and have overhead that undercuts competitive pricing.

Let me explain with two examples.

Stanford construction

Years ago, when I was general counsel at Stanford University and Stanford Medical Center, we were doing over $1 billion in construction in a short span of years. Our architects and contractors were people and companies with whom Stanford had longstanding relationships, some for over 100 years and with whom we would continue working in the future. But problems sometimes arose as inevitably will happen with any construction, be it remodeling a kitchen or building a new hospital.

For lack of any place else, the disputes typically came to the general counsel's office. As I used to say in speeches, few if any of the issues were legal. What we needed to do was figure out where various parties had fallen short and how then to adjust the pricing. Finding those answers would most efficiently draw upon the expertise and methodologies of project managers, accountants, architects, and engineers – not the skills and methodologies of lawyers. Taking depositions and arguing in front of judges or even arbitrators are expensive alternatives and not readily adapted to solving these kinds of problems.

So I used to say, find me a multi-disciplinary team that could review our files and those of our service providers. Take two weeks, maybe a month at the most, and I'll pay the team $100,000 to tell us and the other parties how best to allocate the liabilities. Let's assume they would come back and say something like: the architect's plans were terrific but had some design flaws, so 20 percent exposure there; the general contractor did good work but failed to properly supervise some of the subcontractors, so 30 percent exposure there; and the remaining 50 percent of the costs were because of all the undocumented change orders from Stanford.

I think we all would say, fine, you've done what is needed and we then would adjust the pricing among ourselves.

But I'd then go back to this MDP team and say, here's another $100,000. Put into place a system that will better monitor and manage our construction projects going forward. Use best practices you've learned from similar matters and companies. And then I'd go one step further. Here's another $10,000 to $25,000. Every six months, come and audit the systems you put in place. Are we following them or are we starting to make costly mistakes again? And if our construction managers are finding some better approaches, incorporate them into your systems for us and even for your other clients.

Given our total construction costs, this alternative MDP approach would be a fraction of what traditional dispute resolution entails for Stanford and entities like us. Plus, since donors often helped cover our shortfalls, they used to regularly tell me that they would personally donate funds to implement these sorts of procedures.

European food company

I was in London several years ago and had lunch with Richard Susskind, author of *The End of Lawyers?*.[1] That evening, I had dinner with a long-time friend and his wife. He owns and is CEO of a major food processor in Europe. I told him about my lunch with Susskind and also about the Association of Corporate Counsel's "Value Challenge"[2] and asked what his company was doing about its own legal costs.

"Oh, lawyers," he replied. "We don't use them anymore." He then told me about a UK company that provides a comprehensive service at a fixed price for HR and health and safety, the two areas that used to account for 95 percent or more of his legal costs. This entity largely doesn't advise his managers but instead performs the functions directly. That is, they write his company's employment and health and safety manuals; they update the manuals as they see trends among their many other clients and their interactions with regulators; they train his senior people as well as the workforce; and they regularly audit for compliance.

And then my friend noted, almost in passing, "Oh yeah, and if we get sued, which almost never happens anymore, they have some lawyers who handle it". This result is very similar to what we achieved at Stanford with our major outsourcing/partnering years ago. When expertise is properly brought to bear, the number of disputes falls dramatically – at Stanford, after five years of the partnering/outsourcing, we had half the litigation as we had had the prior decade, even while our legal costs had been reduced by 25 percent.

My friend in the UK loved the fact that what once was a major uncertainty in his annual budget – the costs of compliance and disputes – was now a fixed line item. It also was a huge benefit that the few disputes that now arose internally or with his regulators were quickly resolved and that he and his management team could instead focus on running the company.

If you think about it, what this MDP is doing for my friend and numerous companies like his is what law firms and in-house corporate counsel also largely do: we are monitoring for trends and deploying our expertise. But the MDP is able to directly solve problems, something we lawyers aren't authorized to do. Put more starkly, the MDP has the authority and expertise to be proactive, not simply reactive.

Platforms

I've already noted why law firms and accounting firms may not be the best platforms for offering MDP services.

One way they might become more workable platforms would be to give internal practice groups much greater autonomy in determining how best to staff themselves and price their services. Many practice groups would likely find they could actually increase profitability by reducing hourly rates, something that is anathema to most law firm chairs. Profitability would turn instead on a practice group increasing efficiency, as well as the number of clients served. In most cases, this also would mean pricing services at a fixed or similar approach and not by the hour. Rather, hours would be used, if at all, solely as a way to monitor internal costs of production and where the goal would be to continually reduce the cost of hourly work units as well as the number of work units needed to accomplish a task. A related goal would be for the practice group to be financially rewarded by clients for outcomes versus costs of production.

The idea that a law firm or accounting firm should be run top-down by a dominant CEO works against all of this. Rather, law firms and accounting/consulting firms are more like a hotel that provides space and basic services to its residents and otherwise stays out of their way.

Another analogy is to a university or medical center. Yes, we at Stanford or Amherst or Cleveland Medical Clinic all have a brand, and we watch for any departments that might not be maintaining the expected quality. But otherwise each academic or medical department is fairly autonomous. That is, what an English department pays a professor is quite different from what is paid to a dermatologist or heart transplant surgeon. And by the way, although the dermatologist's billing rate may be a fraction of the heart transplant surgeon's billing rate, the department of dermatology is often far more profitable than the surgery department. High billing rates do not necessarily equate with high profitability.

Subsidiaries of law or accounting firms largely won't work either because of the "heads I win, tails you lose" syndrome. If the subsidiary is barely breaking even after the parent receives its payments for overhead or profits, the subsidiary's workers likely will stay. On the other hand, if the subsidiary is highly successful, its leaders and workers eventually will want to be spun off or will leave on their own. The issue is made even more complicated since a lot of the target market will be clients of other law or accounting firms who aren't going to send work to the subsidiary of a competitor.

In reality, most MDPs will find the best platform for them is an independent entity that they own and control and is devoted solely to their and maybe one or two related practices. As a result, everyone in the entity will have a common bond of expertise. There will be much wider career opportunities throughout the organization – for example, a sales manager could someday be CEO, something usually not possible at a law or accounting firm. The technology staff will no longer be in some remote department that is stretched thin and often doesn't even understand what individual units do. Rather, technology staff members will be fully integrated with the business and will often see major ways to improve efficiency and client satisfaction. Technology staff members might even be placed on site with various clients to integrate what the MDP is doing for those clients, including where the services are being offered on a total outsourced basis.

Privilege

Legal privilege will still be important and will be a problem for MDPs. It's why law firms that are devoted to litigation may have a very strong future. But to be competitive, they will need to learn how to quickly and efficiently match up with a specific MDP, assess the exposures, maintain privilege, draw upon the MDP's expertise and then develop a successful advocacy plan.

Something similar will be needed internally at a company. That is, if some portion of litigation is kept in-house, there will need to be sufficient separation so that privilege can be maintained. That might mean an executive vice president for risk, compliance, and solutions, to whom the general counsel/head of litigation reports, but where their interactions are carefully set up in order to preserve privilege.

Conflicts

I've already discussed the problem of conflicts when a law firm and in some cases an accounting firm tries to be the platform for MDP services. The conflicts issue alone will be a serious impediment for law firms to deploy MDP services.

And yes, I know many firms seek blanket conflicts waivers. Most of us general counsel properly won't give such waivers but rather need to consider the issues case by case. I always bent over backwards to let my law firms represent other entities. But as I said, it isn't solely a question of the rules of ethics, it's also how this comes across to my senior managers. If I tell them this outside law firm is just like me, and truly devoted to the company so my managers can share highly sensitive information, imagine how I come across if, a few months later, those same lawyers are on the other side against us. And no, my telling my senior management that the firm (supposedly) has an ethical wall in place doesn't satisfy their concerns. For the law firm to properly maintain standards and deploy its expertise, its lawyers need to share information. So even if they don't name my company in their practice group and other internal meetings, they actually are sharing information about my company.

Possible transition

There may be a useful way for law, accounting, and other professional services firms to transition from their current structures to what I have suggested is ahead for MDPs.

That would be to informally divide the firm's current professional groups between those that are best positioned for offering MDP services versus those that will continue to provide the current and more traditional services. For example, a group within the environmental department at a law firm might be separated into the advisory and compliance group and allowed to develop a different approach to that practice. This might include different pricing, including fixed prices; the addition of more nonlawyers, some of whom might be paralegals but many of whom might carry titles such as "compliance specialist," "advisory assistant" and the like; and over time the development of very different interactions with clients. As noted in my discussion about the European food company, these entities might often provide their services on a total outsourcing basis for many companies.

Similar approaches might be tried in labor, benefits, tax, and similar areas.

Parallel to those units would be groups that handle litigation or other types of disputes in a given substantive area, with the common feature being that privilege is very important to that group's work and that the matters they are handling are being prepared for actions pending before a court or other tribunal. Something similar would be done at the accounting firms in transition and where independence is important for a specific type of work and thus the consulting and outsourcing role is inappropriate.

The law, accounting, or other professional services firm would then monitor how these parallel groups develop, but being in the position to someday spin off the MDPs into one or more separate firms. The original firms might offer support services on contract to the spun-off MDPs, but with an understanding that management would now be entirely separate so that privilege for the legal group, independence for the audit group, etc. can be maintained.

During the period of transition, lawyers and paralegals would have time to decide which career paths make the most sense for them, and the practice groups and the firms likewise would learn during the transition period what works well and what might need to be done differently.

The end result would be something similar to what I have otherwise described. MDPs ultimately would exist in one or more separate entities that specialize in particular areas (HR, environmental, corporate compliance, etc.). What remains in the traditional law firm would largely be focused on litigation and other forms of dispute resolution. Similarly, what remains at the traditional accounting firm would be what is required for independent audits.

I believe this transition is inevitable. The question for leaders at law and accounting firms, as well as general counsel and other corporate executives, is whether they get ahead of the curve or find that these changes eventually are thrust upon them.

This chapter originally appeared in *Future Law Firm Business Models*, published in December 2018.

References

1. Susskind, R. *The End of Lawyers?: Rethinking the nature of legal services*, Oxford University Press, 2008.
2. www.acc.com/valuechallenge/

Chapter 14:

The evolving role of the PSL – past, present, and future

By Ailish Hogan and Lucinda Troostwyk, PSL and KM recruitment specialists at Taylor Root

Background

Traditionally, professional support lawyers were a function of large City firms, providing and updating a central precedent bank, conducting research, and delivering internal training. Following the economic downturn in 2008, PSLs were suddenly considered a luxury, and many were made redundant. From 2013 onwards, the PSL market began to recover, and the role was re-established in many firms, albeit transformed from its previous guise. Now, at a growing number of firms, the PSL function is seen as a fundamental part of the business infrastructure and a critical contribution to both internal and – increasingly – external efficiency and productivity. The profile of the role has undoubtedly been raised, with real importance now being attached to its function.

As the PSL role has developed, the job title has too been adapted. This chapter refers to the role of the "PSL", but these developments apply to a wider range of roles, including knowledge development lawyers, KM attorneys and practice development lawyers – a reflection that the position has genuinely evolved beyond that of a support function.

How has the role of the PSL evolved?

Previously, PSLs would work reactively to fee-earners' enquiries and their needs for training. Increasingly, the role of the PSL requires a much more proactive approach. Rather than just preparing and delivering internal training, PSLs will work as part of a wider KM function to identify and efficiently develop the training strategy of the firm. Larger projects and strategic initiatives relating to the KM function will be part of their remit, whilst continuing to deal with day-to-day enquiries.

A key part of the PSL role is now to encourage fee-earners to re-think their approach to KM, and to ensure that processes around knowledge sharing are in place and observed. The PSL will frequently now form an essential part of a well-structured knowledge management team, saving the fee-earners time and increasing productivity by enabling them to focus on billing. There is also an increasing degree of interaction for a PSL with other teams in the business (e.g. marketing, business development, IT), and what was predominantly an internal facing role is becoming more client-focused. A strong and highly responsive KM team – of which the PSL frequently forms an integral part – ensures knowledge is consistent, shared, and constantly evolving with the business to meet clients' needs and demands.

More than ever, PSLs are able to develop and shape their own role; partners and group heads are now encouraging PSLs to carve out their ideal job and are always interested in new areas of expertise and innovative concepts. As the scope of the PSL role has expanded, some of the larger PSL teams now have their own support team in place – knowledge paralegals and knowledge and information officers, for example, are becoming more common.

The last couple of years have seen a noticeable increase in newly created positions. Titles vary, but the premise is the same: to ensure that teams across the firm collaborate and have a shared commitment to the PSL function. There has been a genuine shift from the PSL as purely a support role to existing as a vital part of a law firm's infrastructure.

The range of roles now on offer, from entry-level PSL to global head of knowledge, makes this area a genuinely attractive alternative to fee-earning.

How have internal perceptions changed?

Previously, the role of a PSL was largely standalone, with little interaction with members of the firm outside the specific practice group. Now, however, PSLs are much more integral to the wider firm. Experienced PSLs will often report into partners and group heads and will be consulted on wider knowledge management issues and strategies. PSLs are now commonly working with internal marketing, business development and IT teams and are pivotal in bringing these elements of the firm's infrastructure together cohesively. A former candidate of ours has observed:

> *"Eight years ago [in my role as a corporate PSL], I rarely worked with anyone outside my immediate team. It was probably the only thing I missed about being a fee-earner! Now, our internal network of PSLs have expanded so I have a great peer group and on a daily basis I'm working*

with other teams in the firm. I'm really enjoying being such an integral part of the firm, and its been great for raising my profile internally."

What about external attitudes?

PSLs are now expected to be more client-facing than ever and are becoming a valuable resource for clients too. Preparing clients updates on legislative and regulatory changes has long been a part of the role, but most PSLs are now enjoying increased access to clients. Many will now provide training to large FTSE clients on key areas of law. One client of ours has stated:

> *"Twice a year our employment PSL attends our [global banking] client's office to provide updates on recent legislation and market practice. Having an expert who can go in and explain complex legislation and, importantly, its impact in a commercial context – which allows [the client] to avoid pitfalls – has been invaluable."*

Being an expert on the black letter of the law has always been a pre-requisite, but there is now a growing trend for experienced PSLs to be involved in responses to legislative consultations. The level of contributions by PSLs to articles, journals and publications as experts in their field is also increasing, with experienced PSLs regularly being asked to contribute on issues around knowledge strategy.

What are the challenges?

As the scope of the PSL role has evolved, so too have the challenges faced. Recent advances in technology and the pressure to reduce costs mean that PSLs are now required to keep up-to-date with technological advances, and are increasingly working with IT teams to provide a framework for knowledge management. Becoming a PSL remains an attractive option for many fee-earners, and for good reason. However, in practice areas where PSL roles are scarce (real estate, disputes, employment and tax), competition is often fierce. Those wishing to make the move, particularly at entry level, will need to upskill and expand their capabilities. As well as academic and technical excellence, fee-earners need to demonstrate genuine enthusiasm and interest in a move into a PSL role. Ideally, they will need to be able to point to specific examples of PSL-related tasks they've undertaken alongside their fee-earning commitments.

Existing PSLs, too, are having to expand their skillset to keep pace with the developments in this area. Enthusiasm for knowledge sharing is essential, as is confidence in your own ability and being able to interact with those at all levels. To progress, PSLs now need to ensure that they have a full understanding of how they can add value and convince fee-earners, partners and the wider firm of the importance of knowledge sharing and the PSL function.

As ever, there is a need to be highly organised, but PSLs are now dealing with an increased number of competing deadlines. It's essential to deliver on a daily immediate basis whilst ensuring long-term strategic projects don't lose their momentum. The level of pressure has certainly increased, with one PSL we spoke to stating:

> *"It's always been a role where the ability to keep all plates spinning has been essential – but now there are more plates than ever!"*

How have the career structure and progression prospects evolved?

Progression opportunities and career paths for PSLs still vary considerably across the City. Some of the Magic Circle and larger firms now offer an "of counsel" position, which can be akin to partner level. A number of firms still have a flat structure where PSLs at all levels report into partners or group heads, and others offer a simple structure and reporting line as follows:

PSL – senior PSL/counsel – head of KM – global head of KM

However, as the role and its challenges have transformed, there is a growing demand from PSLs for their employers to provide a clear and defined career structure. Responses to this demand vary considerably at present, and whilst some firms have a lot of catching up to do, what is clear is that firms who are addressing this issue will find it easier to attract new talent and retain their existing PSL specialists. Management at one City firm recently commented:

> *"We are currently developing a career structure for our knowledge managers. They want a clear structure and motivating career prospects – just as our associates have a clear career path to guide and encourage them, so too should our PSLs. We want to encourage this talent and retain this valuable source of expertise."*

At an increasing number of firms, there are genuine opportunities to progress internally, or to be promoted into a lateral move as head of PSLs or head of knowledge management. For PSLs who find themselves in a career cul-de-sac, there are increasingly attractive alternatives elsewhere, providing they can embrace the new challenges and demands in this area.

In September 2018, it was reported in the legal press that one US firm had appointed a PSL as a partner. This is an extremely rare move, but a very encouraging one for those working in this area, as noted by *The Lawyer*: "Few firms bring in PSLs at partner level, with the move representing a possible new career path for lawyers who have not followed the traditional track to partnership".[1]

In terms of remuneration, substantial bonuses are still the exception, but they do exist for high performers. Whilst salaries are certainly capped for standard PSL roles, financial rewards do exist where roles include a more strategic element. Firms are becoming increasingly aware that if they want to overhaul their PSL function, they will need to offer an attractive remuneration package. In the future, firms who genuinely buy into the PSL function and are prepared to invest in it will reap the rewards.

What does the international landscape look like?

In the US, the PSL role is a relatively new concept, and the market is this area is much less developed than in the UK. At the moment, these roles primarily exist in New York-based finance teams as KM attorneys.

In the Middle East it is a very small market; PSLs generally only exist at the larger international firms and often work in a more general KM capacity, with there being an expectation that PSLs will cover more than one area of speciality. The Asia & Pacific market is very similar, with only a small number of roles existing in Singapore, Hong Kong and Australia – again, with PSLs being expected to cover multiple practice areas. Commonly, a "transactional PSL" will provide support to the corporate and banking teams, and a "disputes PSL" will advise on arbitration, disputes and regulatory areas. Generally, the ratio of PSLs to fee-earners is much lower than in the UK.

So whilst internationally the role of the PSL isn't yet evolving as rapidly as it is in the UK, it is a developing trend and the level of investment in this area is likely to increase.

Conclusion

As we have seen, the nature and scope of the PSL role has evolved, which too has had a noticeable transformative effect on the demands made of the PSL and the challenges they face. A key element of the PSL role is now to promote and ensure collaboration across the firm, and PSLs need to encourage fee-earners, partners and other key teams in the firm to make a shared commitment to knowledge sharing and development. To progress, PSLs need to gain the respect and confidence of not just their practice group but of the wider firm, demonstrating that the role of the PSL is key to all of them.

However, whilst job titles and career structures still vary from firm to firm, the list of desirable characteristics for a PSL are consistent: Efficient. Effective. Dynamic. Concise. Proactive. Adaptable. Innovative. Motivated. Forward thinking. Commercial acumen.

The role of a PSL is clearly more demanding than ever before, and this development is likely to continue. However, for those wishing to pursue a career in this area, the rewards are there. Transparent and progressive career structures are becoming more common, making the PSL route a challenging and interesting alternative to fee-earning. Exciting opportunities exist for those who embrace them.

This chapter originally appeared in *The Evolving Role of the Professional Support Lawyer*, published in September 2018.

Reference

1. Moloney, R. "From PSL to partner: Kirkland breaks new ground with Weil hire", *The Lawyer*, 5 September 2018. Available to access from: https://www.thelawyer.com/from-psl-to-partner-kirkland-breaks-new-ground-with-weil-hire/

Chapter 15:
The evolving law department – what the future holds

By Patrick J Lamb, founder of ElevateNext Law and vice president of Elevate Services

No business *wants* to have a law department: businesses have law departments because they *must*. Of late, there has been much conversation about law departments evolving from a necessary evil, the department of "no," to valued part of the business. Even as some law firms are evolving in this manner, the pressure on corporate law departments is growing geometrically, perhaps exponentially. Change is happening faster than ever, and general counsel who are not keeping pace will be challenged to have a plan to do so and begin executing it sooner rather than later.

While change in business is accelerating, change in law departments – not to mention their law firms – is not happening anywhere near fast enough to keep up. Most CEOs are focused like a laser on digitizing their businesses, fundamentally transforming it. This is happening with incredible speed: 85 percent of business decision-makers see the transition happening in just two years, and fear financial jeopardy or losing ground to competitors if they cannot execute on this issue.[1] However, nearly 60 percent of these CEOs are concerned their businesses "do not have the sensory capabilities and innovative processes to respond to rapid disruption."[2] Businesses can ill-afford to have a law department that does not keep pace with the businesses they serve. It is unlikely CEOs will have patience with law departments that do not have a strategy for keeping up.

Think about that for a moment. Corporate law departments need to significantly accelerate their ongoing transformation *just to keep up with their businesses!* Few departments have developed their modernization plans, and fewer still are executing those plans. There are, however, a few "test lab" law departments that provide a glimpse into the future. Within the past year, Univar general counsel Jeffrey Carr announced his "moonshot" goal of reducing legal spend in his $8 billion chemical distribution company by 50 percent. A year ago, Microsoft announced it would be shifting away from the billable hour for most engagements. Both Carr and Microsoft's deputy general counsel, Neal Suggs, have spoken about creating new types of relationships to handle their respective company's legal needs. Their approaches are worth studying and emulating.

Understanding the role of the law department in a modern business

The present

The critical issue facing law departments is growing demand. As companies change, grow and globalize, the legal challenges grow. As technology rapidly advances, the gulf between business and law grows wider at an accelerating rate. Famed economist Herbert Stein once posited that "if something cannot go on forever, it will stop."[3] Law departments simply cannot continue without materially changing their approach.

Since they began, law departments served several functions, but the two most important were cleaning up messes made by business units and serving as the company's interface with law firms that were performing the company's legal work – sort of a cross between a janitorial service and a dating app. The economic pressures of the past decade forced law departments to reexamine their relationships with their outside counsel and make more informed "make v. buy" decisions. These decisions resulted in law departments expanding and bringing in significant amounts of work to be done by lower-priced in-house lawyers, to the detriment of outside firms. But little was done to address the "janitorial service" nature of law department workload, and now the perception is generally that little of the remaining work done by outside counsel can be economically moved inside. The challenge corporate law departments now face boils down to the simple matter of supply and demand: the demand for legal resources continues to grow rapidly, but the supply of internal resources is not rising correspondingly; the labor arbitrage model of shifting work from expensive resources to less expensive resources has largely run its course or is, at best, a short-term solution.

Modern law departments – the ones that intend to keep up with their businesses – will challenge the conventional wisdom and develop strategies and practices which defy the fundamental rules of supply and demand that relate to departmental operation.

The future – an overview

The next generation of law departments will have five essential components. First, to address the "janitorial" problem – cleaning up after problems created by the operation of the company – the legal department will embed lawyers in each of the business units in sufficient number to help critical decision-makers make better decisions. What's a better decision? One that makes the business unit successful and reduces demand on the law department.

Second, the law department will become disciplined at requiring other parts of the business to perform the operations they need to instead of letting those business units transfer their work to the law department. An example of this is contract drafting and negotiation. Most companies have sales personnel secure agreement on price, quantity and delivery date, and then toss the matter to the law department to formalize into a contract. While the law department should own the contracting process, the operational, technical and financial aspects of the corporation must own their respective components of the contract. For example, a contract to sell a product that must operate deep in the ocean has commercial, technical, financial and legal components. The commercial and technical departments are in the best position to know whether the company can perform, and the finance or accounting department is in the best position to know whether it can do so profitably. The legal department addresses the risk to the company if it fails to perform.

Third, the company will also employ modernized process development. Most tasks performed by the legal department have been done before, but nevertheless will involve time and energy to figure out how to do them again. Developing refined processes, supported by checklists, saves time and ensures consistency and quality in the service delivered. The future involves creating those processes and checklists.

Fourth, successful law departments will focus relentlessly on prevention. To that end, various data analytics will play a significant role. Analytics will provide insight into risks created by acquisition, foreign operations, and even employee performance variations. It will involve more mundane data such as quantifying the amount of time lawyers spend on various tasks – for example, some departments spend considerable time answering questions about contract meaning or about credit and bankruptcy issues. The data gathered about this issue will help general counsel allocate resources that can be used to reduce those areas of demand.

Finally, the modern law department will fundamentally change its relationship with its legal vendors, both law companies and law firms. Without fundamental change, law firms and companies will not make the investments needed to develop the technology the legal department needs – there will be no economic incentive to do so. And because few law departments have the resources to develop the necessary tech, they will not be capable of self-funding. A major Catch 22. As a result, the nature of the relationships will have to change from a series of simple transactions – "handle this matter" – to something far more collaborative.

The future – a more detailed look

Changing law departments is hard work. Damned hard. The same goes for changing law firms and law companies. No one who decides they need to be ready for the future should embark on the journey expecting smooth sailing. Indeed, expect the opposite – a bumpy ride, complete with setbacks along the way. But believe in the vision and learn from those who have started building this road before you.

1. Embedding lawyers in business units

One of the advantages in-house lawyers have over outside counsel is that in-house lawyers know more about the company's business. However, when one digs deeper, we learn that while this relative advantage is true, the depth of in-house counsel's knowledge is often not as comprehensive as it could be. In-house counsel may not be at key business meetings for operating parts of the business; they may not have a high level of familiarity with products, methods of operations, procedures and policies, strategies, research and development, financial issues, and so much more.

In an ideal world, there should be a "business unit lawyer attached to the hip of the unit president or other chief officer," and the lawyer would be so plugged in "he or she would have a tissue ready to hand the business unit leader before she knew she was going to sneeze," according to Jeff Carr. True immersion maximizes the opportunities to shape events and decisions in ways which prevent legal problems from ever arising.

The relationships created with day-to-day decision makers will increase the likelihood of the in-house lawyer being consulted regarding decisions that, without guidance, might turn problematic. The best legal problems are the ones that are avoided, of course. Embedding lawyers deeply into business units therefore helps the law department reduce demand by reducing the number of business matters that evolve into legal problems.

2. Requiring business units to assume responsibility for their own work

Because lawyers tend to be problem-solvers, they tend to try to do so for other people. The other people are thrilled to be rid of the problem. In his best-selling book *The One Minute Manager Meets the Monkey*, author Kenneth Blanchard uses this example:

> *In the hallway, an employee raises a problem with the boss. The boss shows some interest in the problem, and quickly the brief discussion has become a 20-minute session, which is abruptly ended when the boss has to attend a planned meeting. The discussion ends with the boss saying, "I don't have any more time now; let me think about it and I'll get back to you".*

The boss has taken the employee's problem – the monkey on his back – and made it his own. The employee has one less problem to deal with, and the boss has one more. Substitute "lawyer" for "boss", and you see the problem.

Contract review is a classic example. Many business contracts involve agreements to buy and sell goods or services. The contracting company's ability to sell a particular good or service is not a legal issue – it is a business issue. If there is a question about the company's technical ability to make a particular product, the company has both a business issue and a technical one. And the issue of whether a price is enough to earn a profit is most certainly not a legal issue. It is the business' monkey. However, in most companies, the monkey – the drafting and review of contracts, with redlines going back and forth with the other contracting party – is taken away from the business and put on the back of the company lawyers. And they willingly take the monkey!

If you start with the goal of only being responsible for legal portions of the contract, you have substantially less work to do. What are legal portions of the contract? Pretty simple really – what happens if the company fails to perform the contract or the other side fails to perform its obligations? Disputes. And within disputes is the subcategory of indemnity risk – what kind of damages might the company be liable for? Many companies have firm positions that they will not accept the risk of consequential damages, or that such damages are capped by the amount of the contract. Regardless of position, that issue is most certainly a legal one.

So why does the monkey typically end up on a lawyer's back? Conventional wisdom is that a contract is a legal document, so therefore a lawyer must write it. Does that analysis hold up? Not at all. An expense report is a financial document, but employees fill out their own expense reports. The accounting and finance department most certainly does not fill out those forms. And thus lawyers have to learn the difference between owning a process and serving as operator. It makes sense for the law department to own the contracting process. That would include what parts of the document are essential; what parts allow for small or large modifications; what approvals are required for deviations from approved language; and, of course, provisions regarding disputes and risk.

Does this business empowerment approach work? Let me start from the standpoint of my experience of having litigated contract disputes for 35 years. More often than not, the business people on one side or both would have little or no informed understanding of what was agreed to – they were strangers to the document. The lawyers often were long gone but the legalese remained, as did the ambiguity occasioned by the fact that the provisions were drafted by lawyers, not the people who would be operating the process that was the subject of the contract. Strike one. Strike two is that contracts are often thrust upon those expected to perform them without any regard for whether the company can actually do so. This happens because the sales personnel are paid based on sales closed, and the operations group only gets the monkey put on its back after the contract is finalized, not when it has the ability to say, "hey, we can't do X and this price" or offer other pushback to ensure the contract makes sense operationally. Strike three is often the bottleneck created by legal review. The review of legal issues can be accomplished in minutes, but the legal review of the rest of contract takes much longer because the lawyers have to learn what the parties actually agreed to and then agree with other strangers to the deal (the other company's lawyers) as to what was agreed upon. Contract velocity – which translates into revenue velocity – can be enhanced by making those responsible for various portions of the contract own the monkey associated with that section.

This type of change to the contract review system challenges companies because people despise change and no one wants their monkey given back to them. The legal team will therefore face change management issues, but the outcome is a significant reduction of demand, both from a better contracting process and from reducing the number of disputes arising from executed contracts.

3. Process development

Process has a bad reputation among lawyers. Lawyers tend to view what they do as "special" and "bespoke," or otherwise customized. Lawyers fear being identified as purveyors of a commodity product. The problem with this line of thinking is that most legal work is the execution of process. Sometimes the process leads to the application of judgment, but oftentimes the execution of the process yields the end result. And every company has processes it must follow. Standardizing work squeezes fat out of the operation, allows for consistent quality, and – in many cases – enables the execution of needed work via application of tech or lower-cost resources.

The key to process development is identifying the steps that must be done and the order in which the steps must be accomplished. An automotive assembly line does not start with the installation of doors. The sequence is important. So is requiring everyone to do the same tasks the same way. If people are free to change the manner they do certain tasks, there is no longer a process, just a suggestion. This is where most law firms struggle – partners are autonomous, after all – and where law companies excel.

Process development is a tough, complex subject that I will not attempt to teach here. Instead, I want to highlight some examples to illustrate the importance of process. Consider an area like trademarks. Most companies have them, and they need to be managed. However, for most companies, there are not so many that you need a full-time inside resource devoted to trademarks. You can hire an outside lawyer to handle all of the work, but at considerable expense; alternatively, you can create detailed processes that a paralegal can execute, consulting a specialized trademark lawyer only when required.

Even an area as random as litigation can be "processified." The right steps, taken in the right order, can assure that insurance assets are fully utilized; that cases are always assessed early and based on the same protocol; and that the risk posed by a case is measured on a consistent basis so the resources allocated to it are proportional. Even something as small as the sequence in which discovery is analyzed can produce risk – the effort to respond is measured and then set against the validity of objections. Only valid objections that relate to a significant effort or risk are pursued; discovery motions are generally lost and are frequently expensive. Most of the time, the expense is unwarranted and could have been avoided.

There is process work to be done in every area of corporate law department practice. A lawyer should never have to figure out from scratch how to do something that he or she has done before, or that someone else in the law department has done previously. Effort should be put into a process and the process should then be shared. The cost savings associated with effective process development is significant.

4. Prevention, prevention, prevention

The law department of the future must reduce the demand for its services, or at a minimum reduce the rate of the demand growth. If growth is not curbed, demand will outstrip resources, putting the law department's essential mission at risk. Some law departments are already experiencing the phenomenon. For most others, it is just a matter of time.

The most effective tool to achieve this goal – prevention – ironically is considered suspect simply because it is hard to measure the value of avoided risk. That concern, however valid, is a poor reason not to implement an aggressive approach to prevention. Consider fire prevention as an analogy. We consider fire-fighters to be heroes, yet every single fire-fighter will urge prevention. The best fire, like the best legal problem, is the one that never happens. In this context, we require smoke alarms in homes; we post fire risk warnings in forests and national parks; and we ban campfires. It is hard to know exactly how many fires are avoided or lives saved by these measures, but we know they are successful. And so, after many years, we continue to utilize these safety measures and employ new prevention ideas when they emerge.

Consideration of a prevention strategy immediately begs the question of what is involved. The execution of a prevention strategy requires a prevention mentality. Few lawyers have this mentality innately; it is a learned behavior. As such, it requires practice regularly enough to become a habit. Because the demands of daily responsibilities tend to prevent the development of new habits, someone needs to be made responsible for implementing the processes and procedures which will give life to a prevention mentality throughout the department, and eventually throughout the business units as well.

Among the tactics a prevention specialist will utilize are root cause analyses on every problem, including litigation, to determine how to avoid them and using the outcomes to create new processes or procedures to avoid their repetition. The prevention specialist also will act as a quality assurance person, ensuring that processes and procedures are followed rigorously. There is more, but this should be sufficient to get the ball rolling.

5. Refining relationships with service partners

Most law departments only have relationships with law firms. That is changing, as more law departments have established relationships with law companies. Among other things, law companies execute the process development discussed in point three above much more capably than law firms. Law companies thrive on developing repeatable processes and then using personnel who did not attend law school and are much less expensive to accomplish the processified work. Law firms tend to eschew this approach because each partner is essentially autonomous, able to do things their own way. Every matter is handled as a unique, stand-alone phenomenon. This approach fails to extract the fat that can be removed by careful processes.

Microsoft – though its move away from hourly billing – has learned that hourly billing interferes with the immersion into the company's business that is needed to create new value. Microsoft deputy general counsel Neal Suggs described the hourly billing problem this way:

> *"In the past, outside lawyers did their best to understand our business, but there was no way they could get the depth of knowledge they would derive from being immersed in it every day. Immersion wasn't an option – the hourly billing model prevented it – so outside counsel delivered legal advice, and inside lawyers had to take the time and effort to figure out how it applied to their businesses.*
>
> *"Businesses can't operate that way anymore. Our industry changes too quickly, our business grows at an ever-expanding rate, and the law is too far behind. We not only need reliable legal advice fast, but we also need it to come to us in a way that's already tailored to fit very particular business contexts."*[4]

The result has been a huge win for both Microsoft and its commercial firm, Perkins Coie:

> *"The first year under the new model was a win for Microsoft and Perkins Coie alike. Perkins Coie hit their goals and received their performance bonus. More importantly, though, the firm's attorneys clearly became more engaged with Microsoft's business. Unshackled from the desire to limit billable hours, the Microsoft team is no longer discouraged from looping in outside counsel for calls, meetings and other opportunities to help them learn the nuances of Microsoft's business. The Perkins Coie attorneys have started delivering legal advice that reflects those nuances and considers the company's needs and goals in ways you wouldn't usually see from an outside firm.*
>
> *"Microsoft gets access to Perkins Coie's deep bench of experts and their broad range of experience, which complement the internal team's deep knowledge of its technology and business. All this makes the Microsoft commercial legal group a more valuable contributor to the law department and to the entire enterprise. The result is a relationship that not only serves Microsoft's legal needs but also helps build value for the business."*[5]

Univar has experienced a similar result. The Elevate and ElevateNext personnel working for Univar have learned the nuances of both the law department and the business units in ways that help us better advise and serve the customer. Without a non-hourly fee arrangement, this immersion and application of the resulting insight would not have been possible.

In addition to better service, both Microsoft and Univar are benefitting from work done by their teammates, Perkins Coie and Elevate, to design technology tools which facilitate even better service and greater insight to the customer into the work being performed by all members of the law department's teammates.

Having been serving clients using non-hourly billing arrangements for more than a decade, I know first-hand that the outcomes experienced by Microsoft and Univar are predictable, not serendipitous. Elevate's experiences with several of its customers confirms the belief that immersion and alignment of economic interests produces powerfully positive results.

Conclusion

Law departments cannot continue as they are in the face of the ever-growing demand for their services. The changes of the past decade have allowed departments to successfully keep pace with the changes in their business, but as change accelerates even more, new strategies and approaches will be necessary. Microsoft and Univar have taken steps that appear to be a productive way to position their law departments for success in the face of this accelerating pace of change in their quite disparate industries. The work has revealed the essentials of a workable strategy for success.

This chapter originally appeared in *Tipping Point: Transformation and Innovation in the Legal Department*, published in January 2019.

References

1. https://www.microstrategy.com/us/resources/blog/bi-trends/17-statistics-showcasing-the-role-of-data-in-digital-transformation
2. https://advisory.kpmg.us/articles/2017/destination-unknown.html
3. http://www.aei.org/wp-content/uploads/2013/06/-130606-media-steins-law_094731626218.pdf
4. https://www.law.com/corpcounsel/2018/12/17/beyond-the-billable-hour-its-not-about-economics-its-about-relationships/
5. Id.

www.ingramcontent.com/pod-product-compliance
Ingram Content Group UK Ltd.
Pitfield, Milton Keynes, MK11 3LW, UK
UKHW021849150926
8657IPUK00005B/159

9 781783 583805